Positive Affirmations Coloring Book for Girls

by

Chloe Nallis

Published by Renuti®

Test Color Page

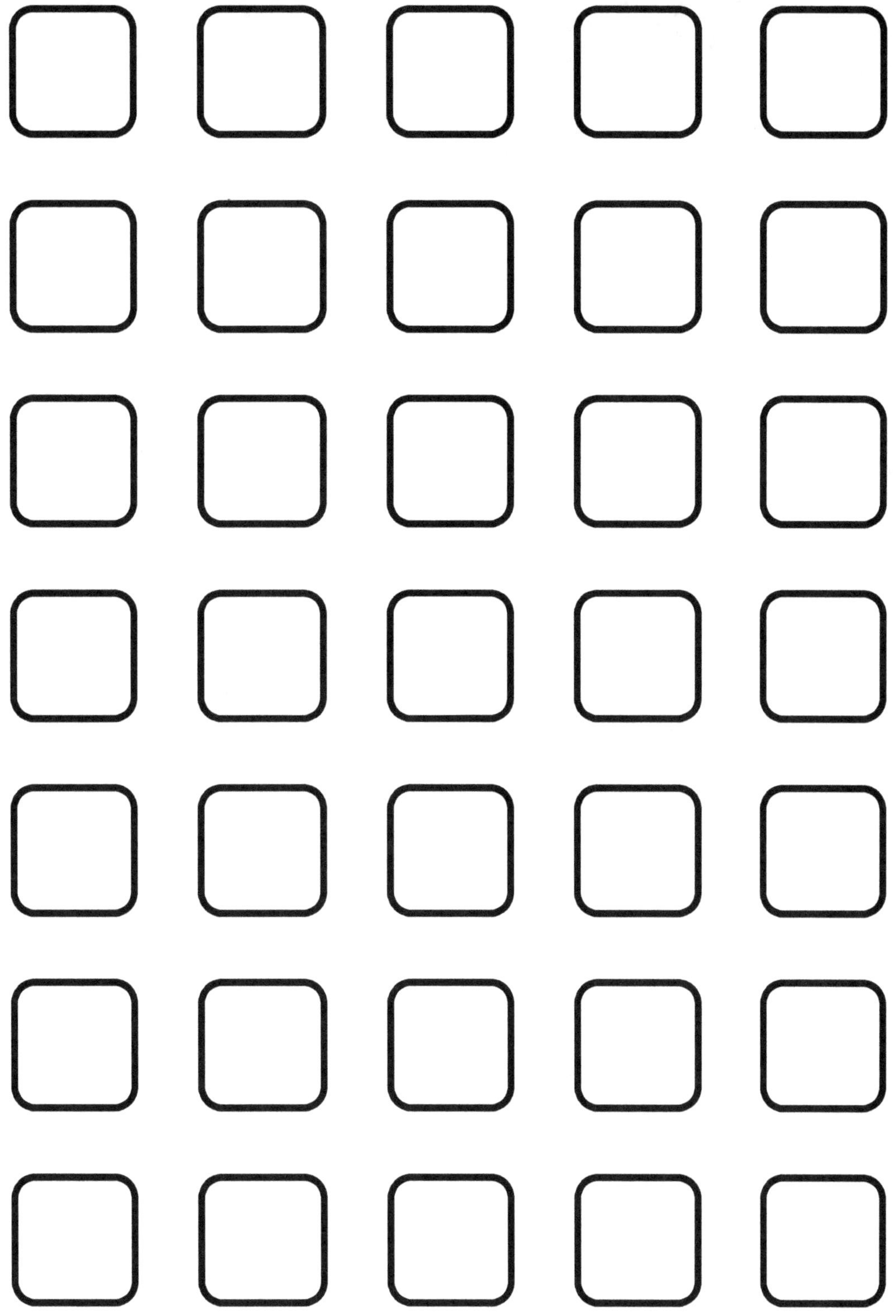

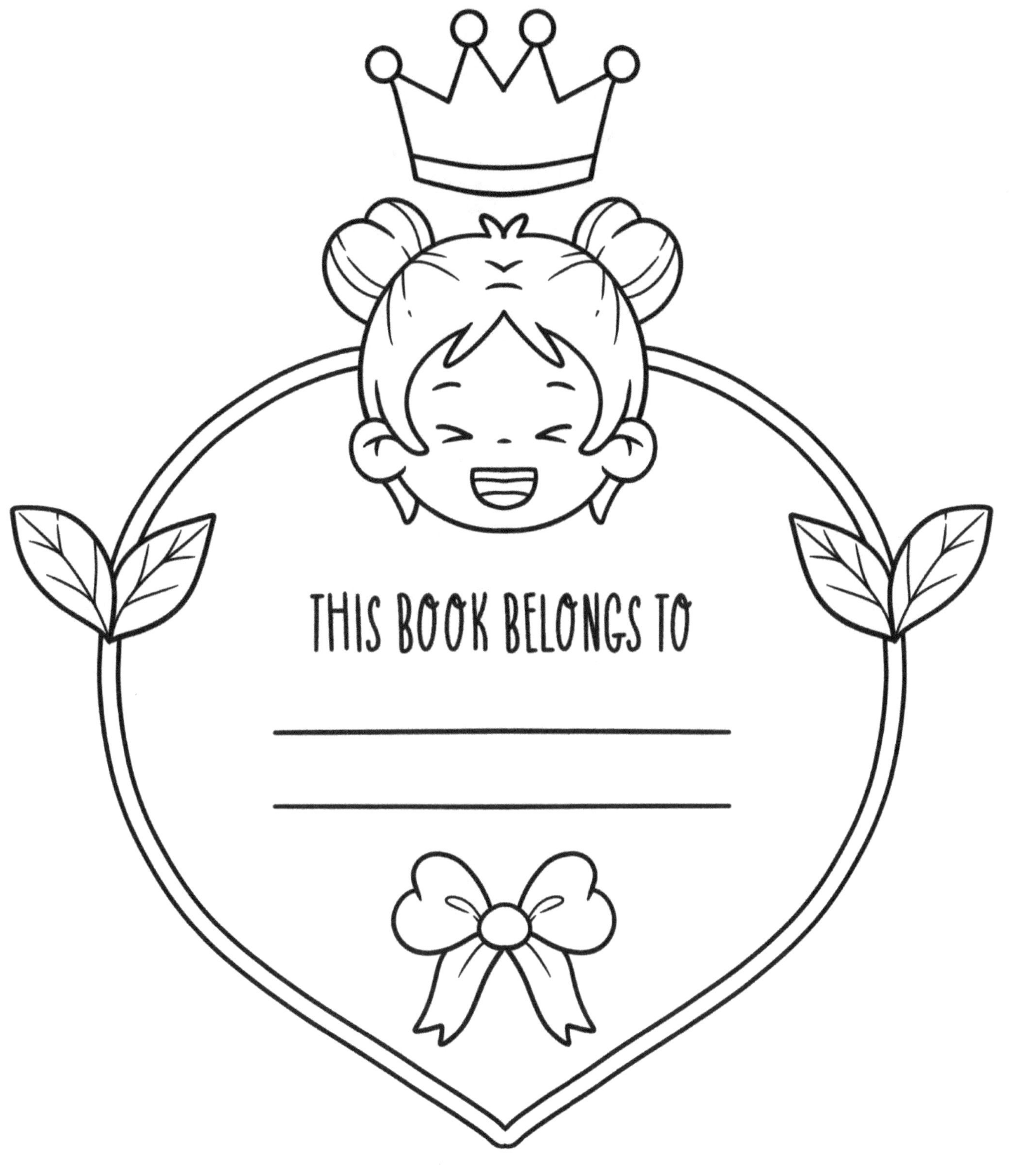
THIS BOOK BELONGS TO

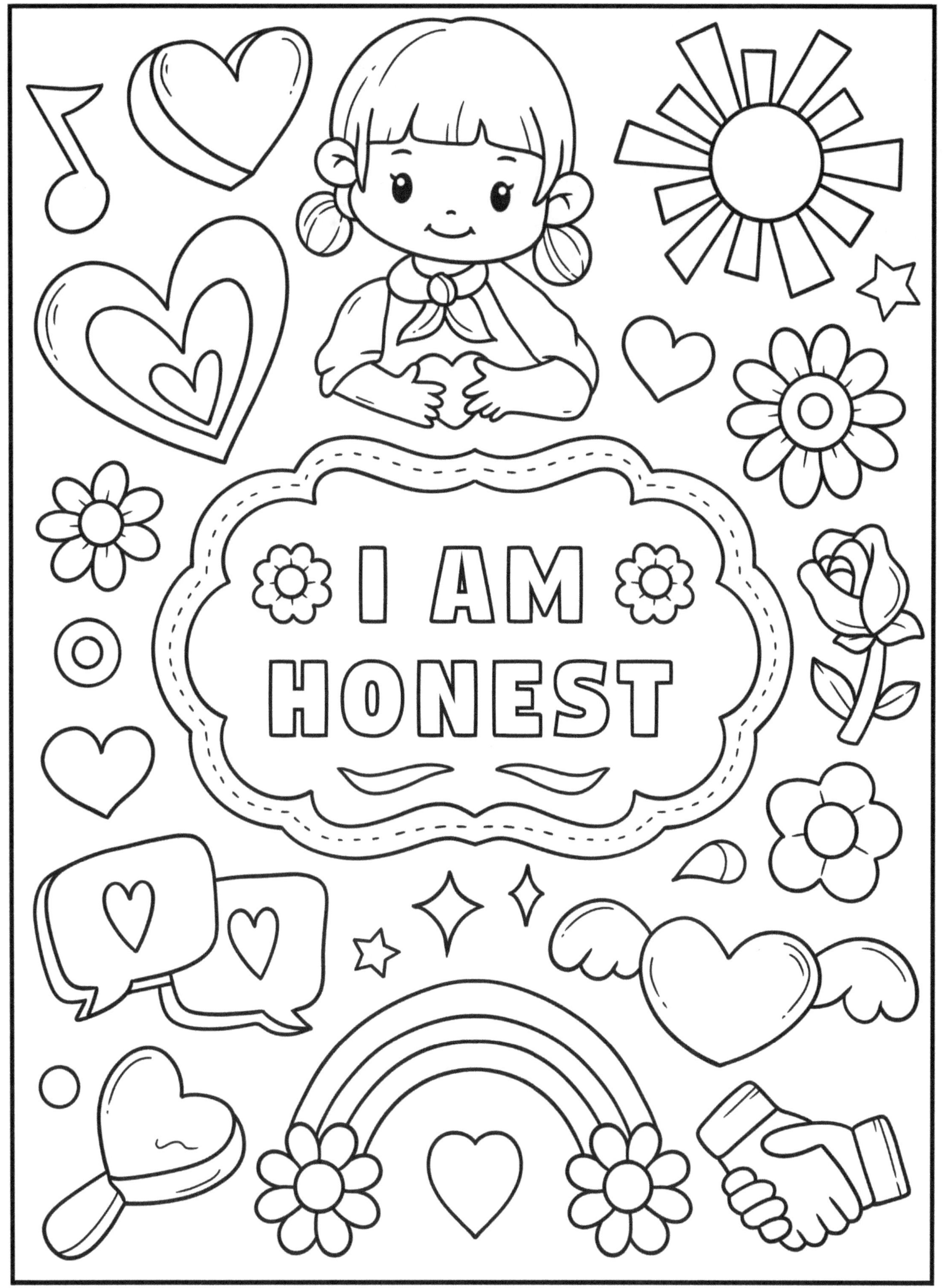
I AM
HONEST

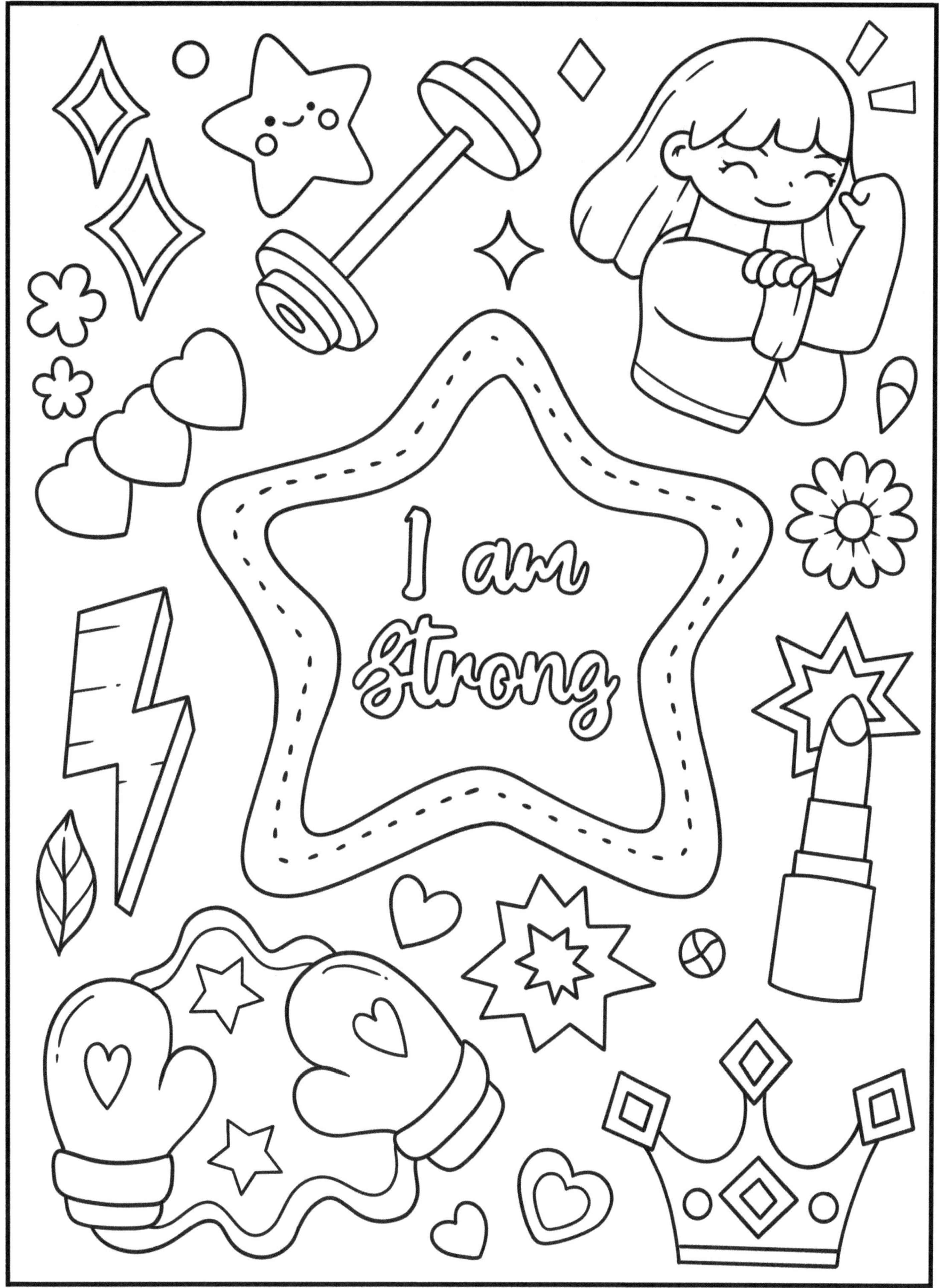
I am Strong

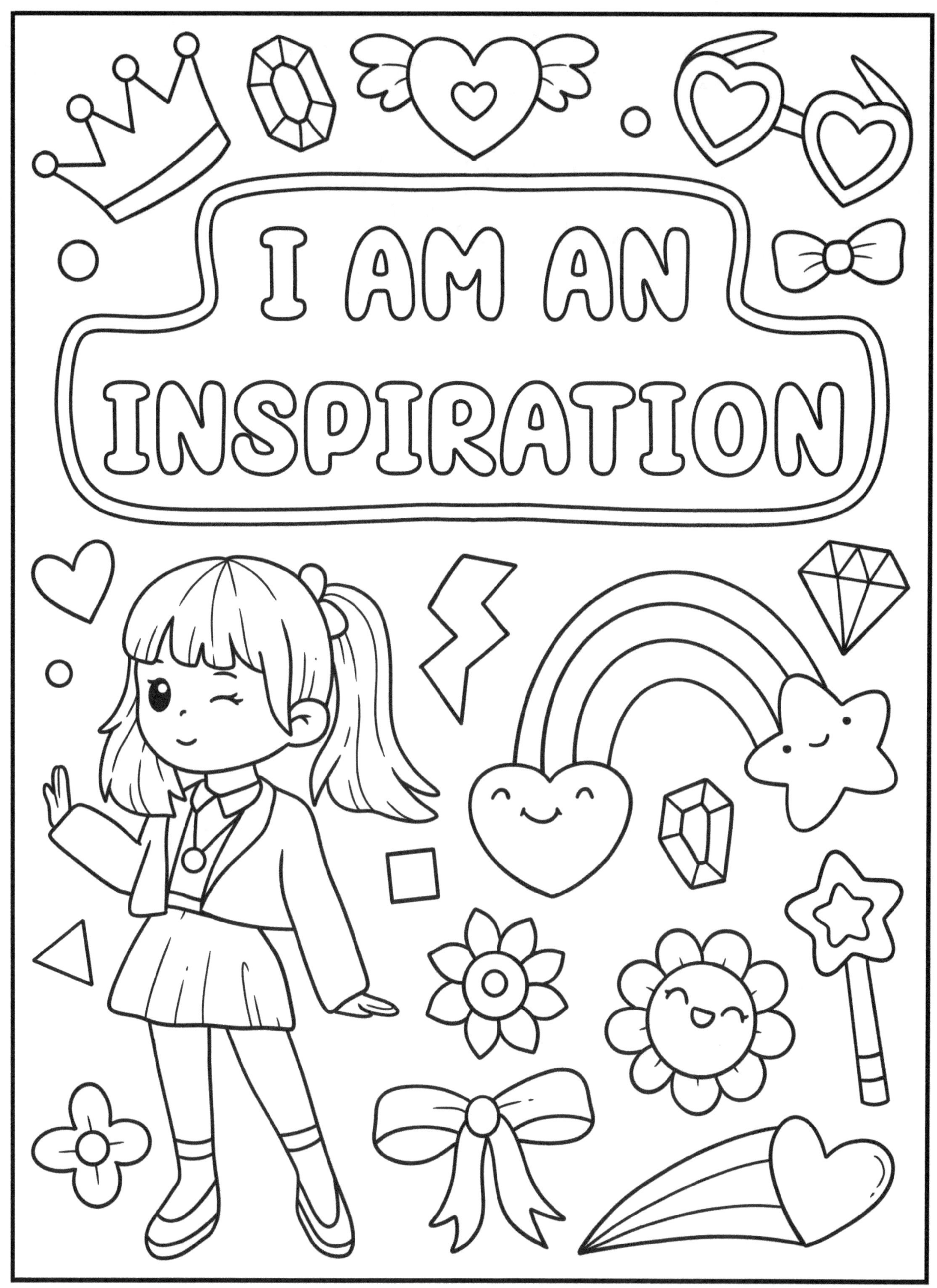
I AM AN
INSPIRATION

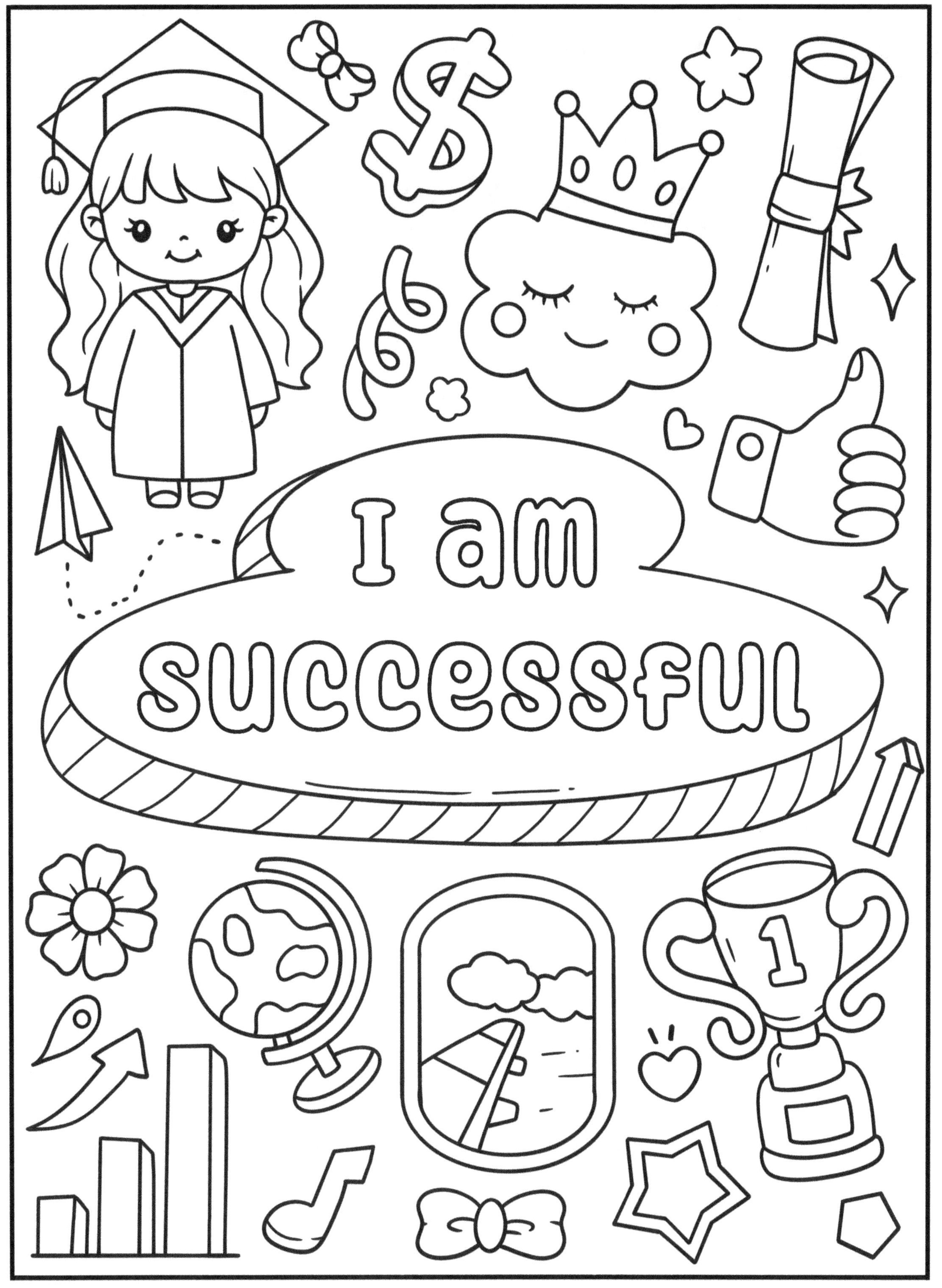
I am
successful
$
1

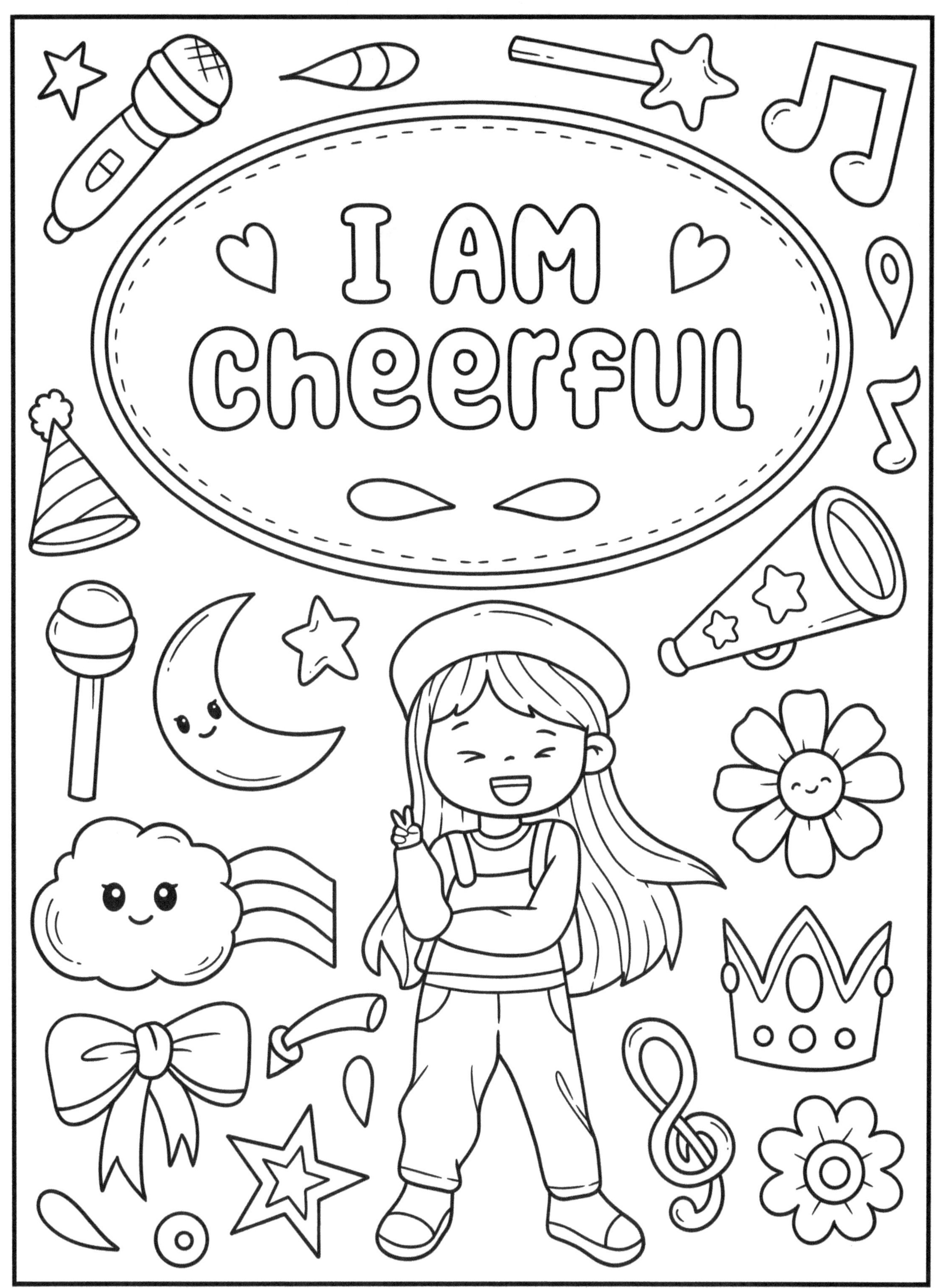
I AM
Cheerful

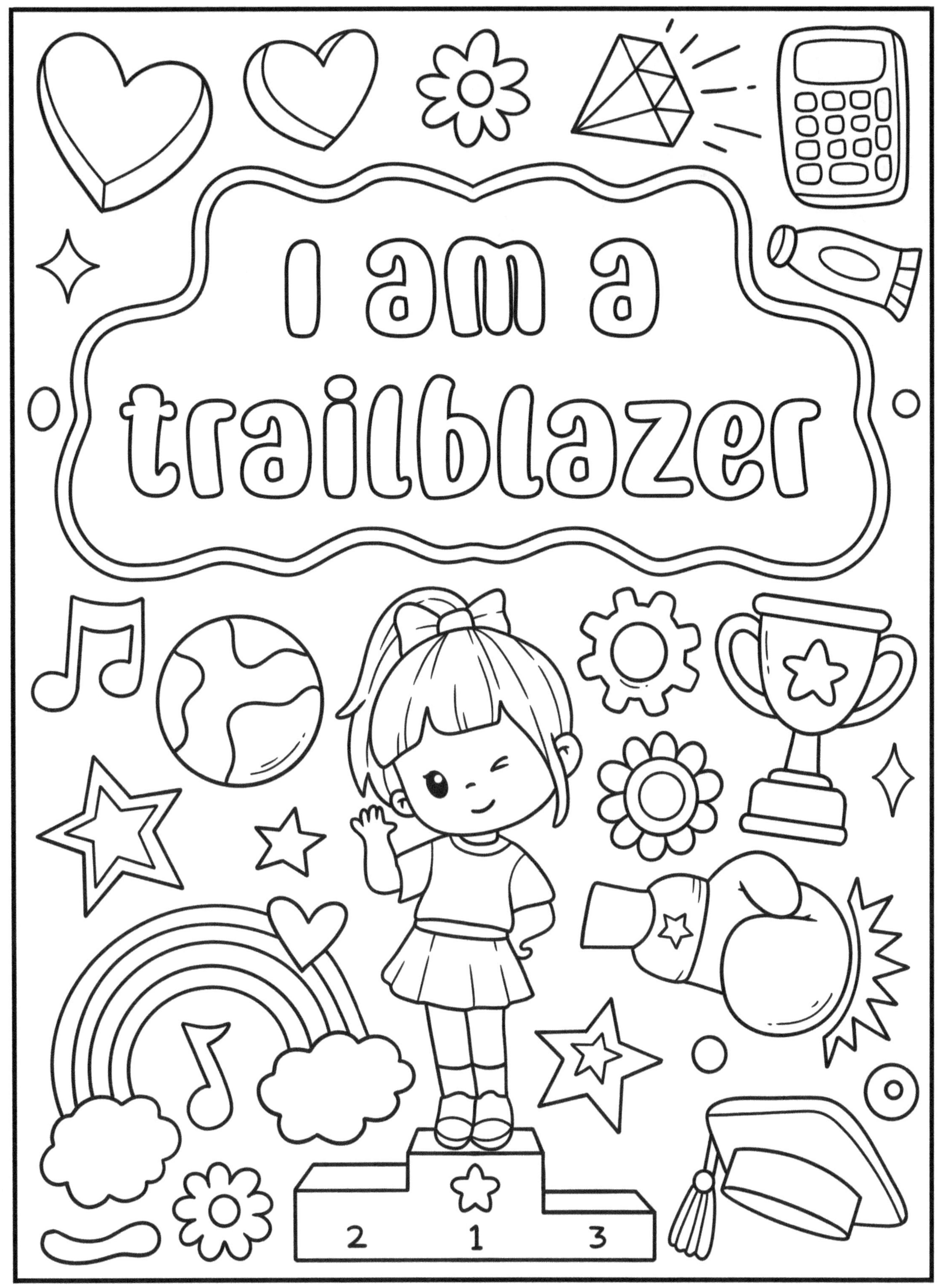
I am a
trailblazer
2
1
3

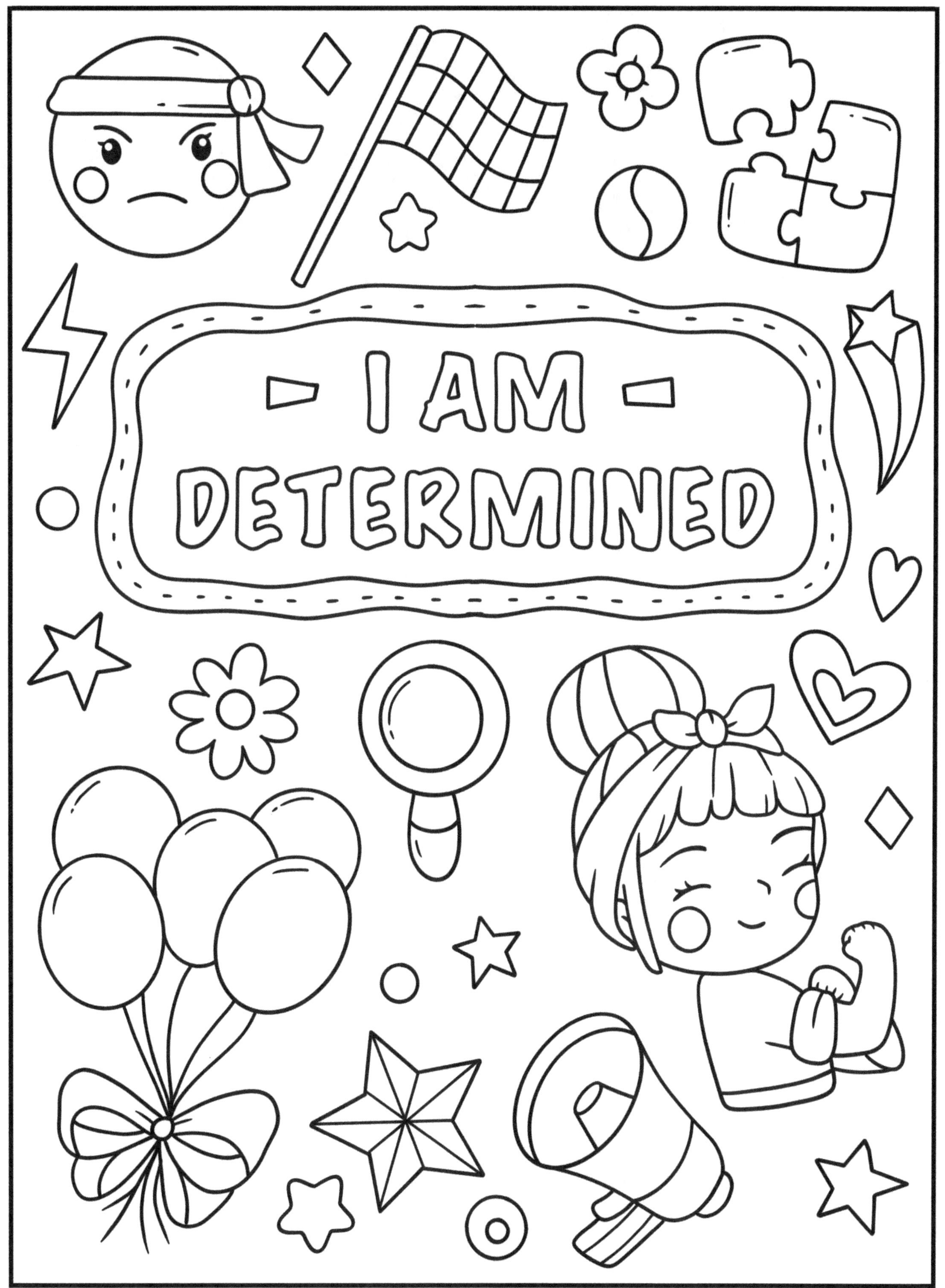
I AM
DETERMINED

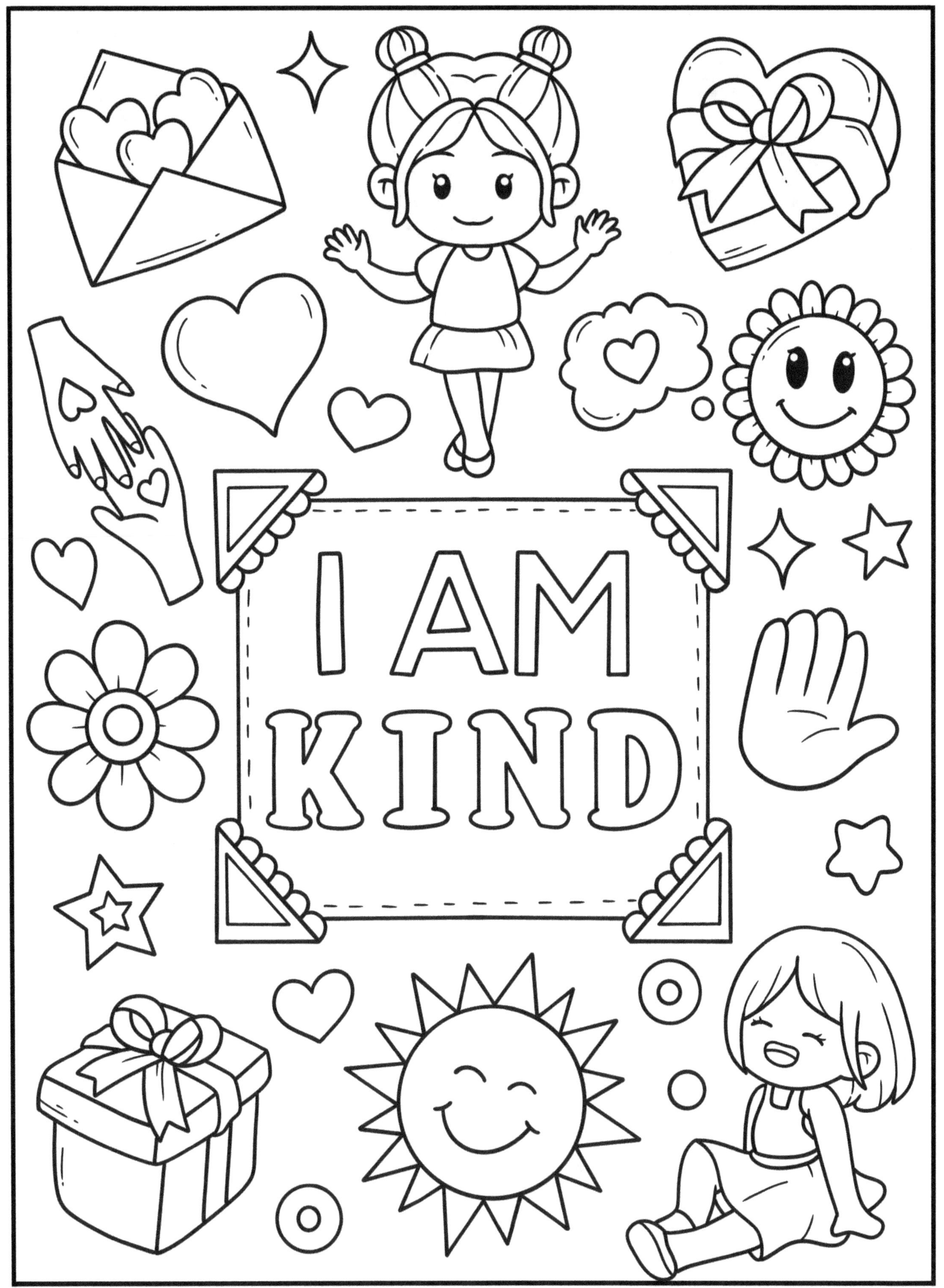

I AM
KIND

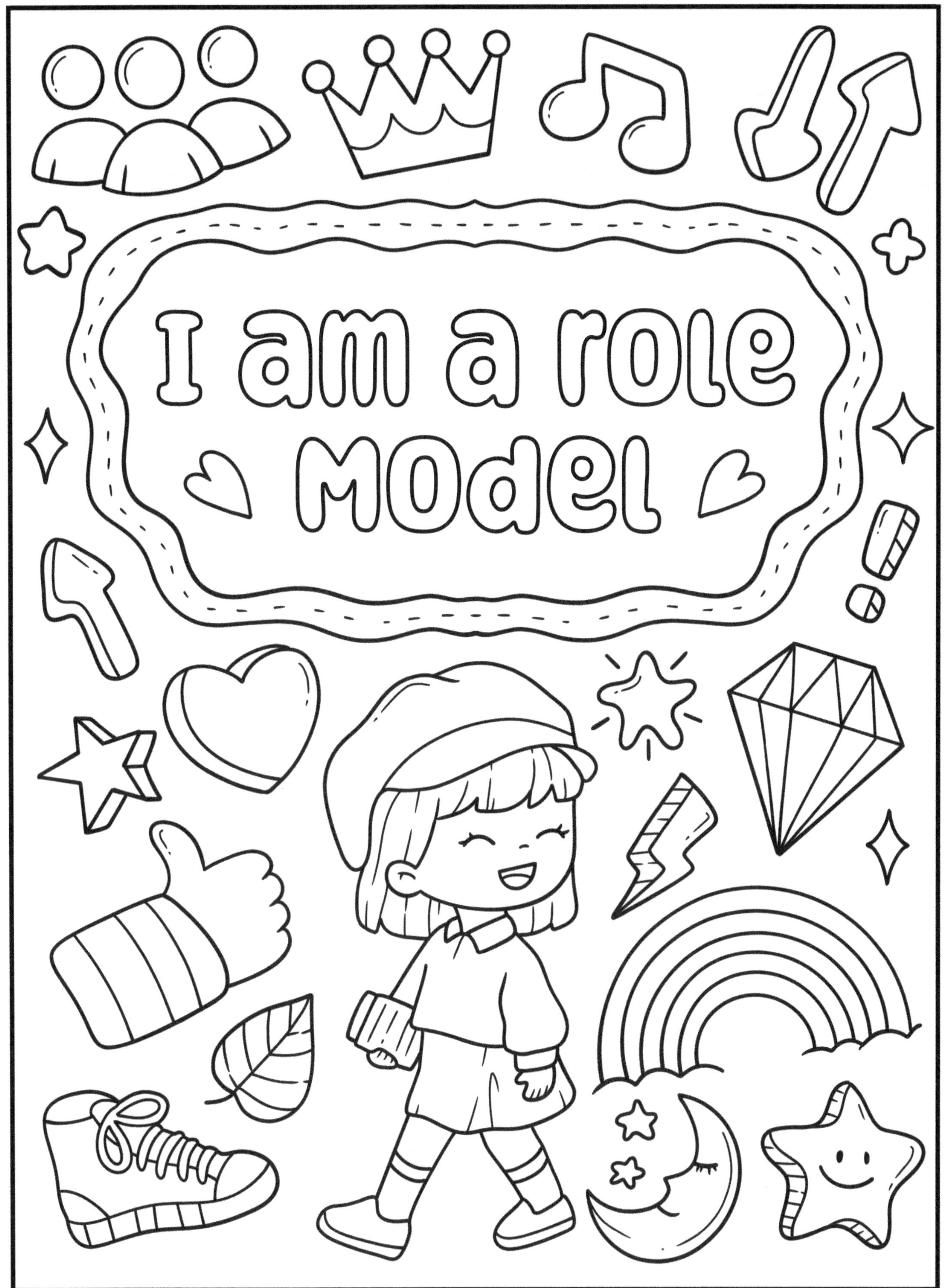
I am a role
Model

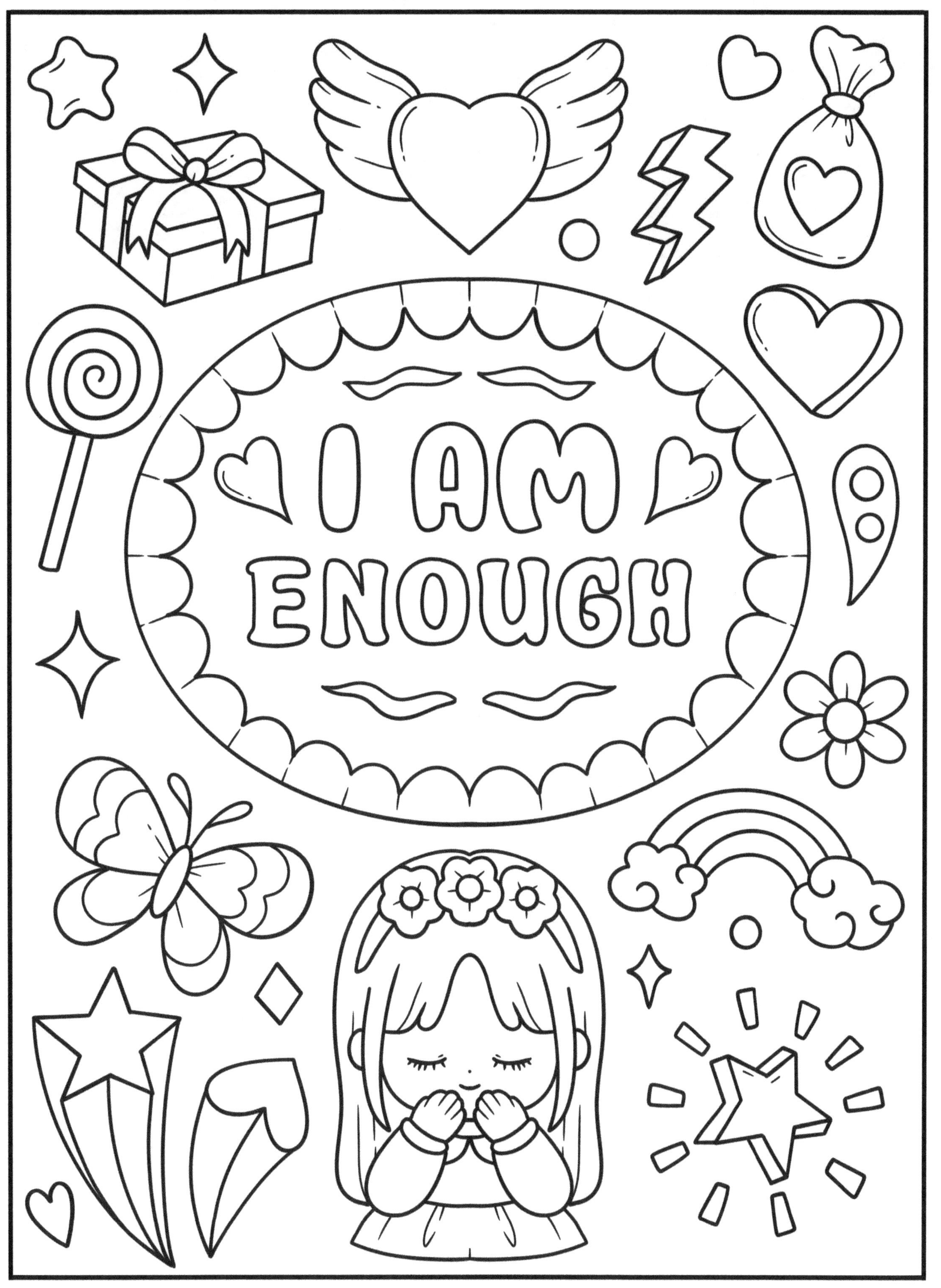
I AM
ENOUGH

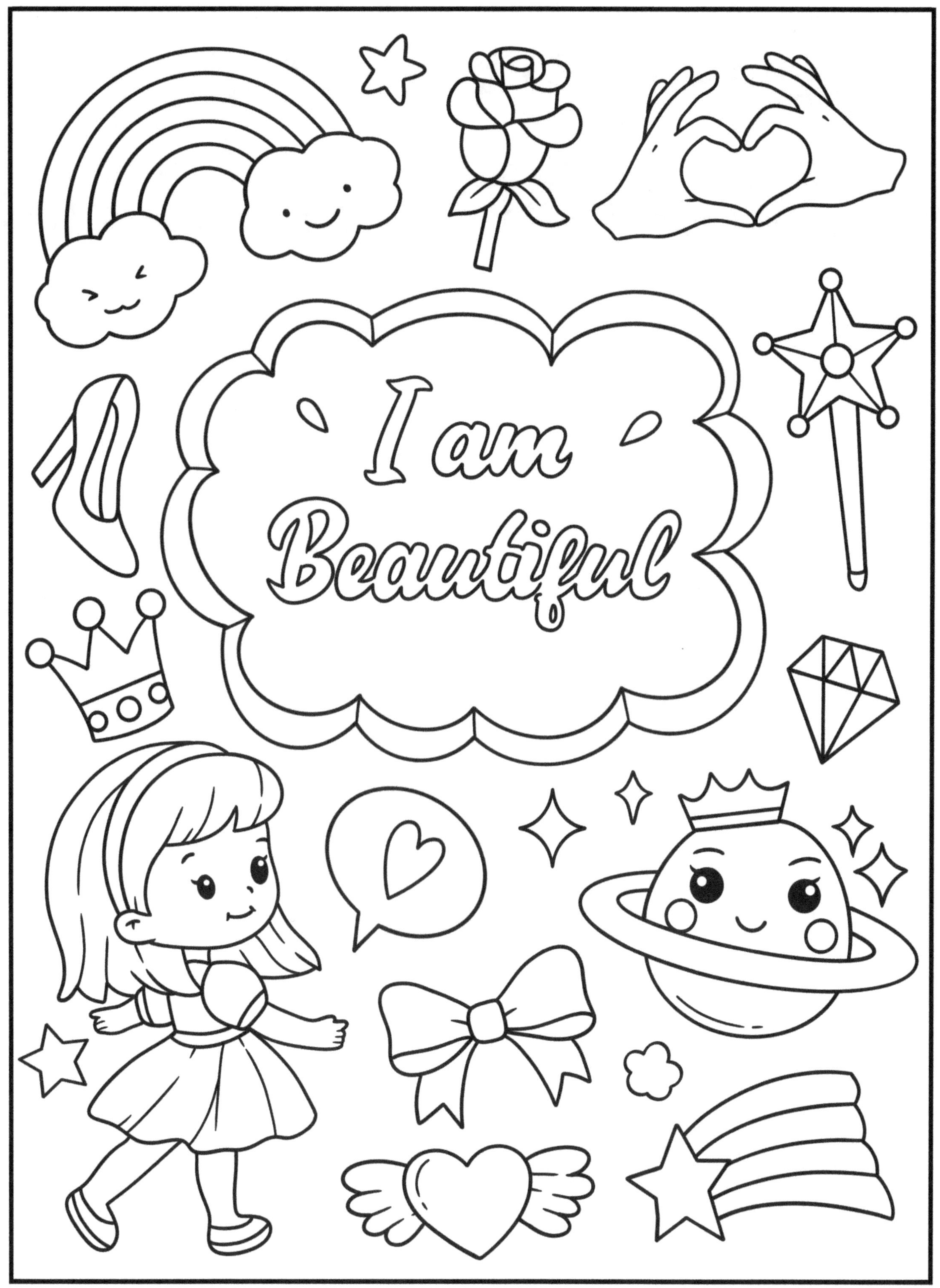
I am
Beautiful

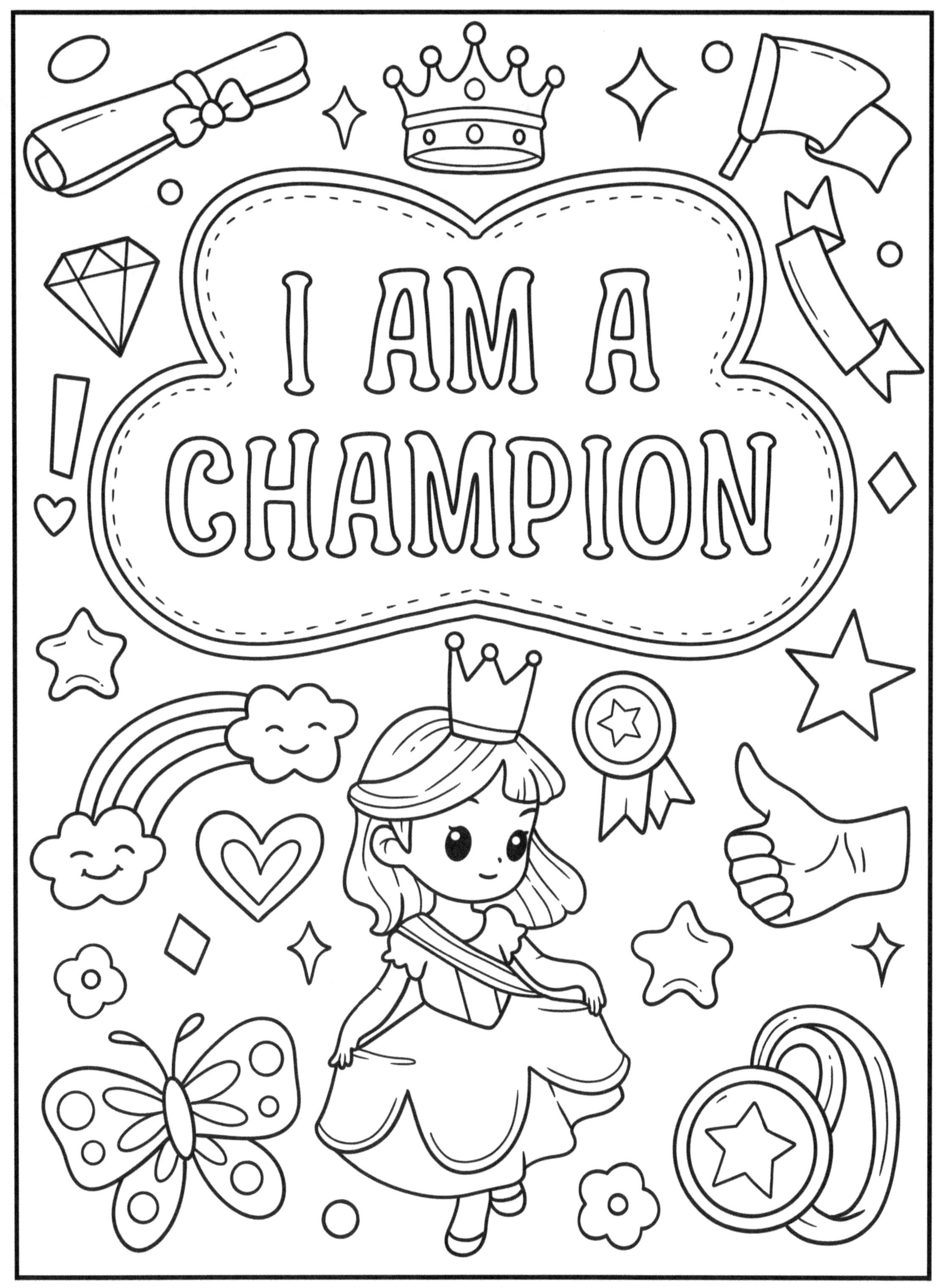
I AM A
CHAMPION

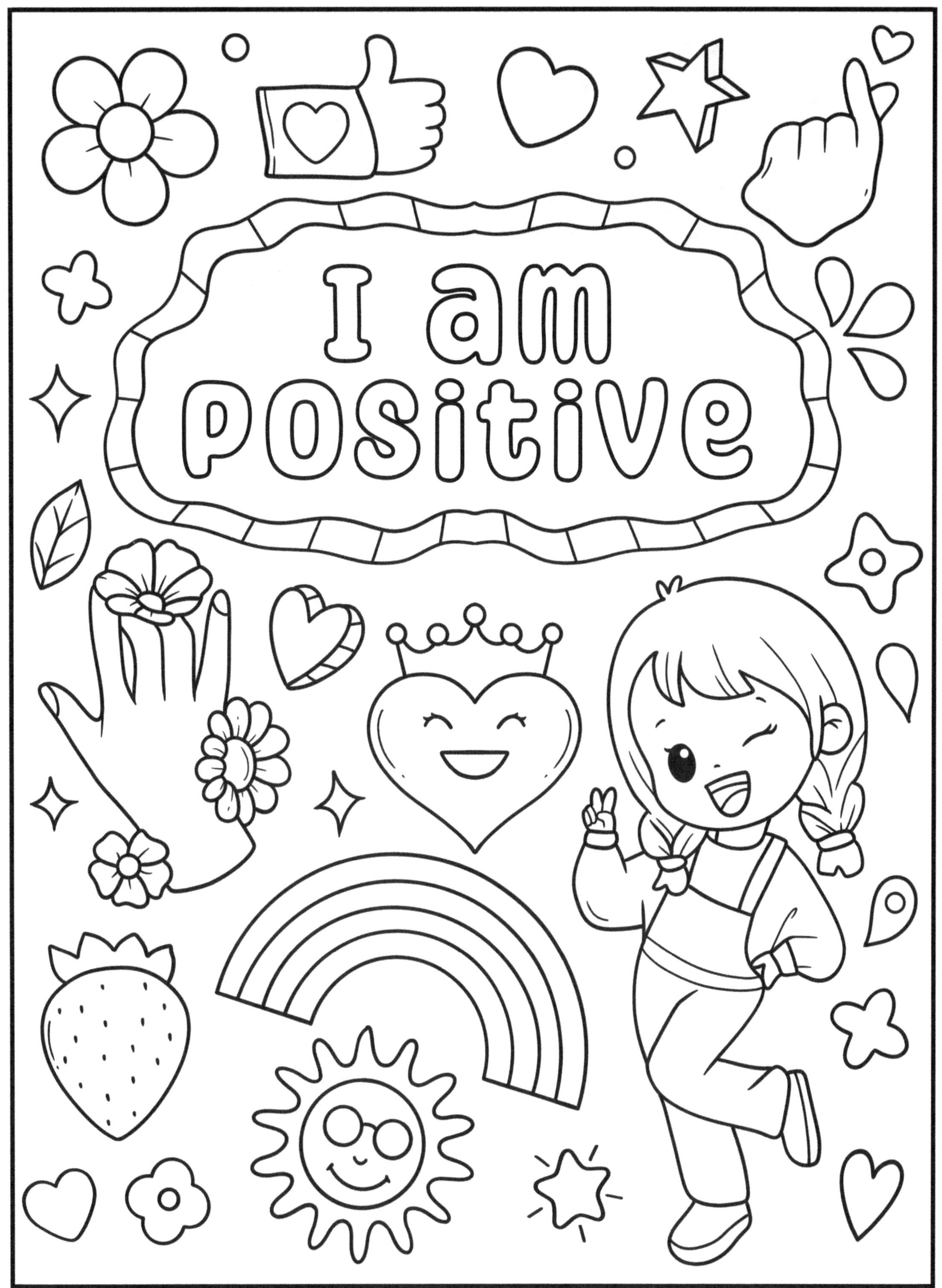
I am
positive

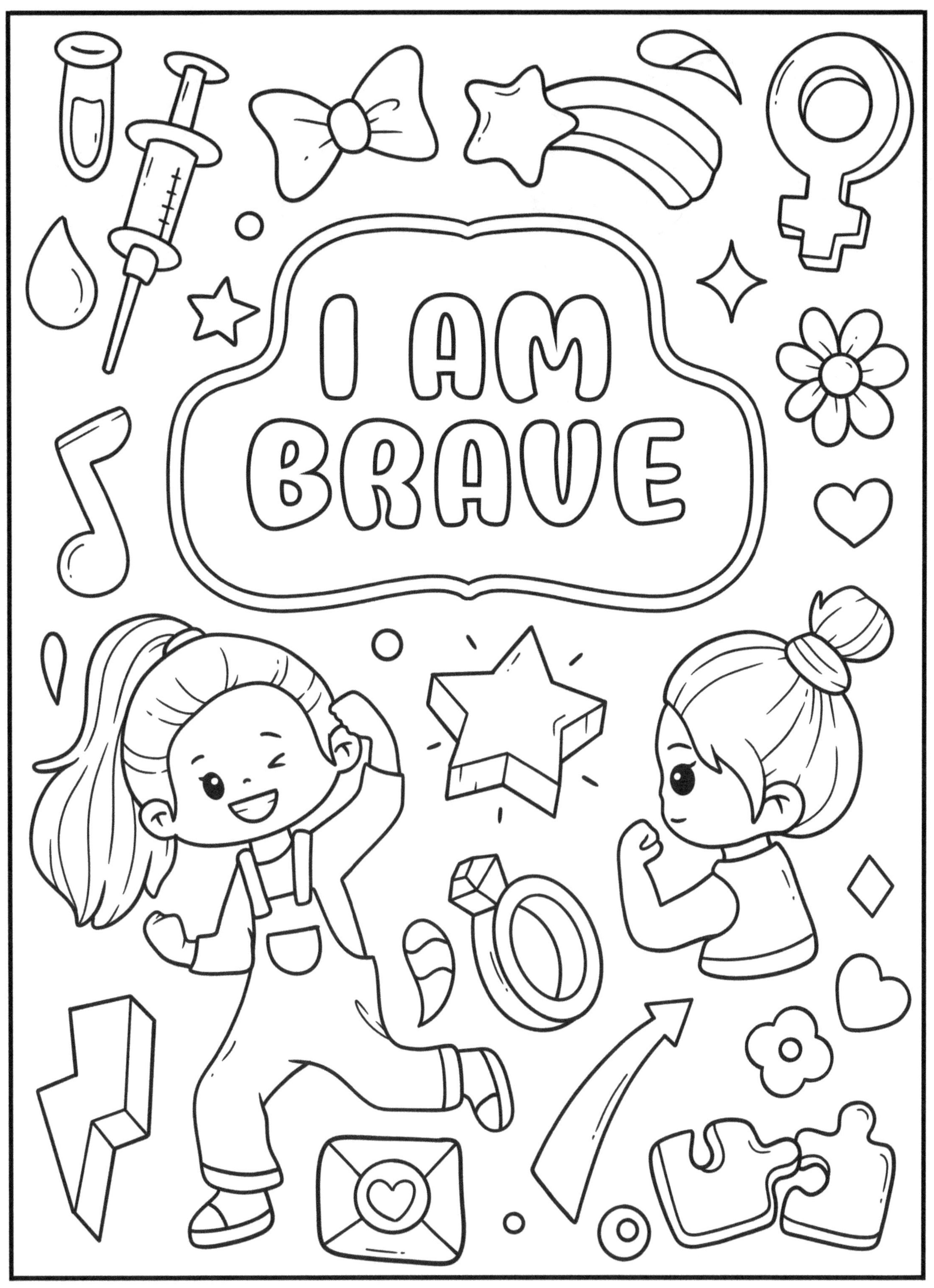
I AM
BRAVE

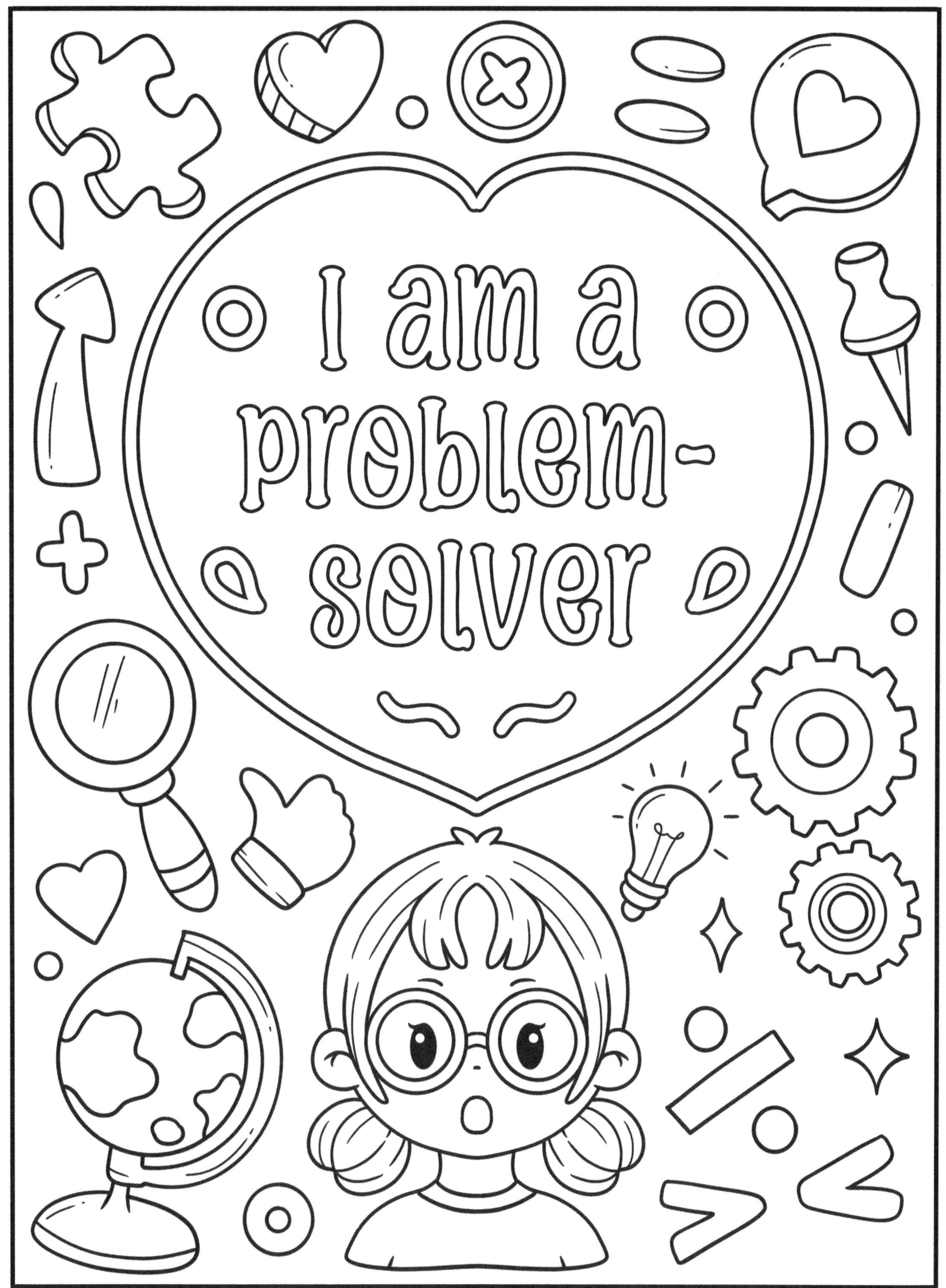
I am a
problem-
solver

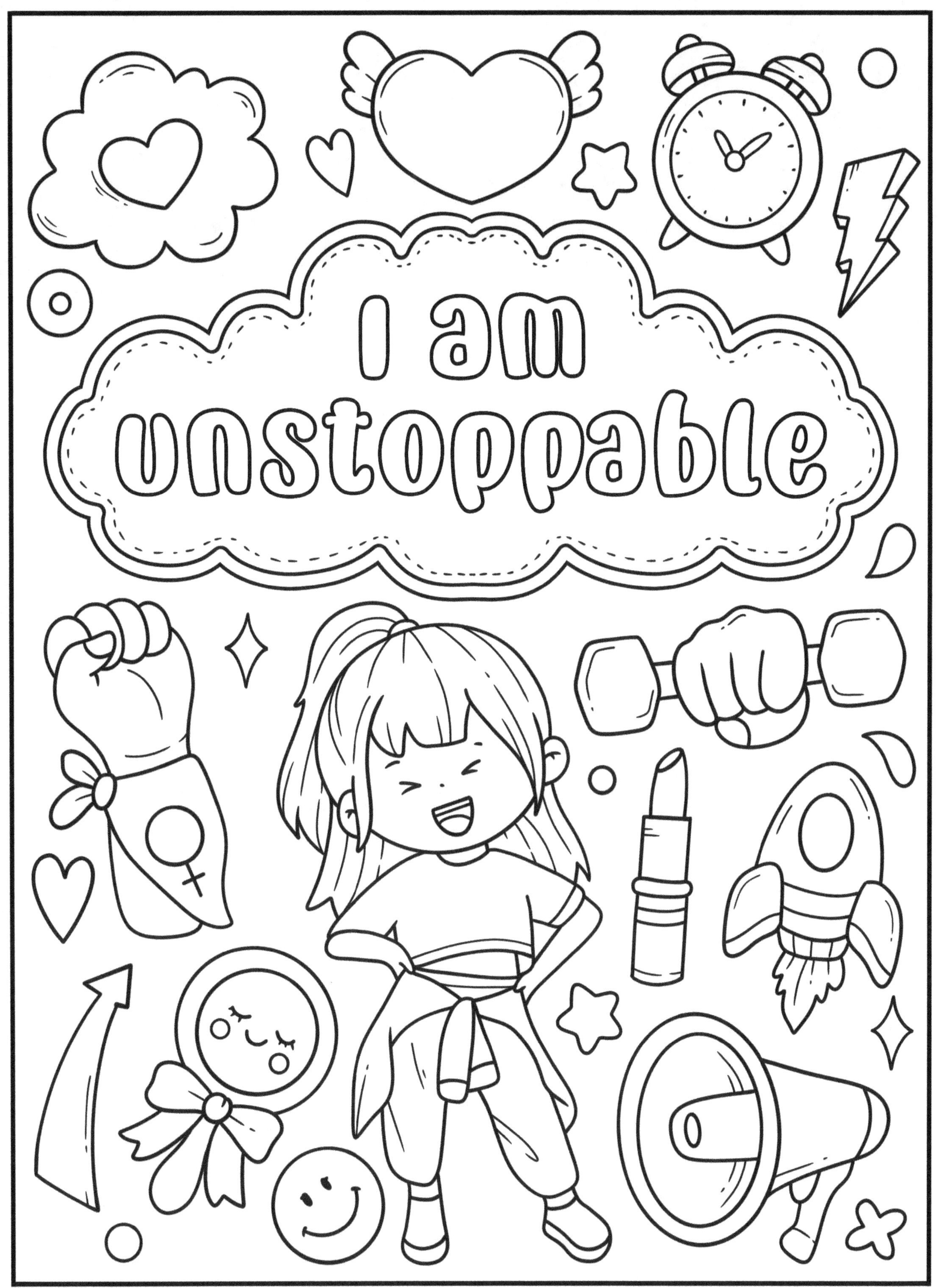
I am
unstoppable

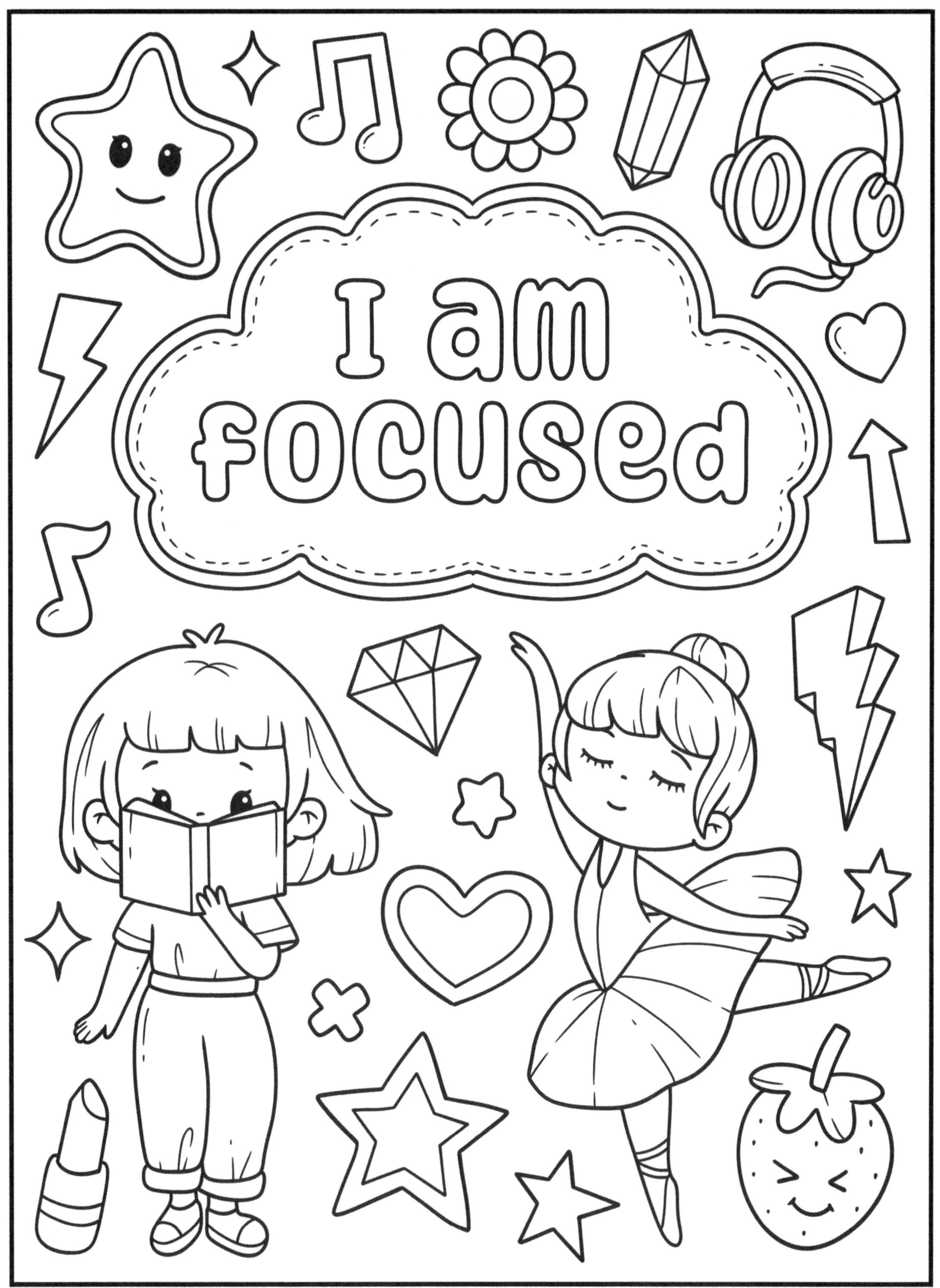
I am
focused

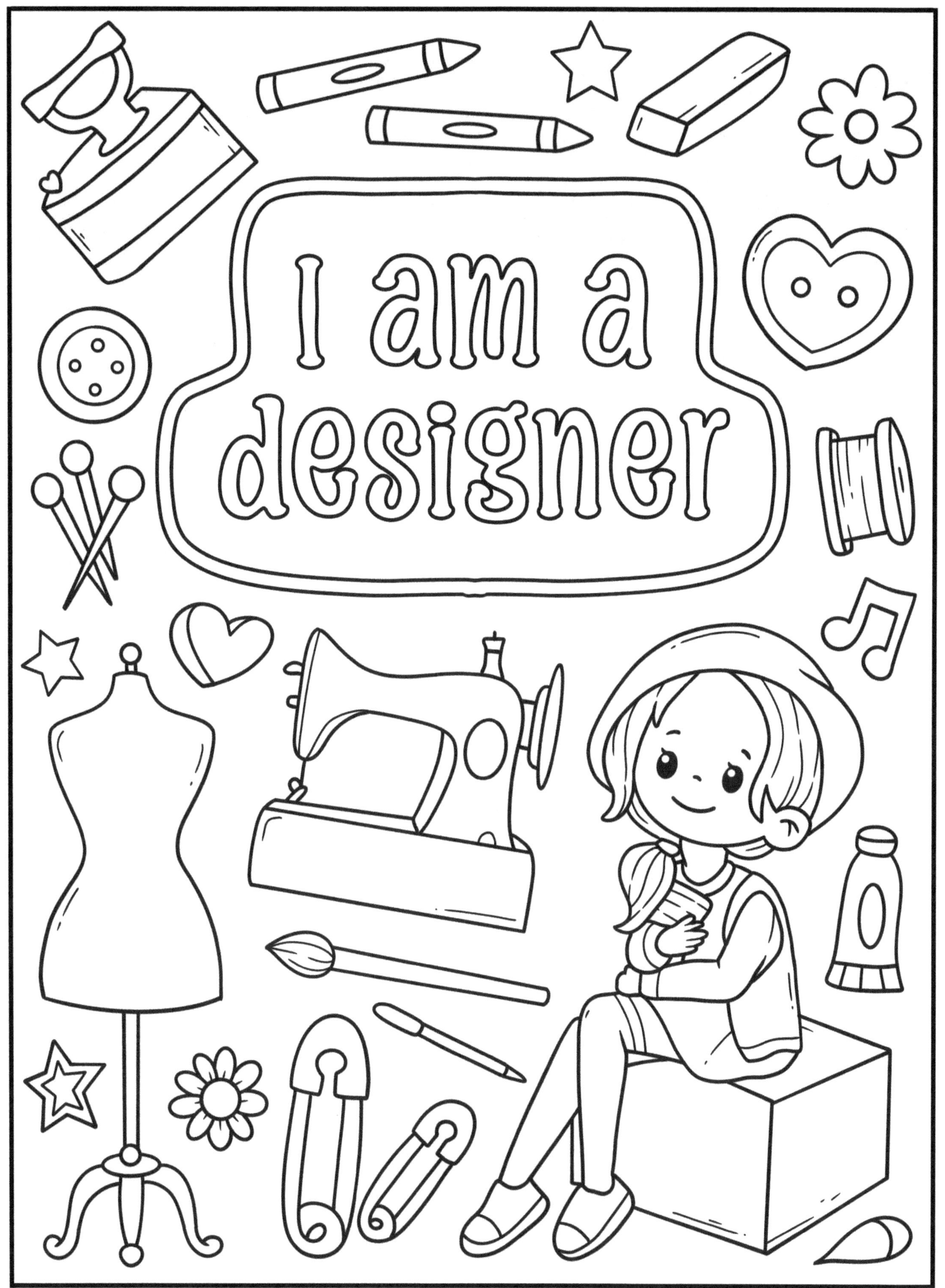
I am a
designer

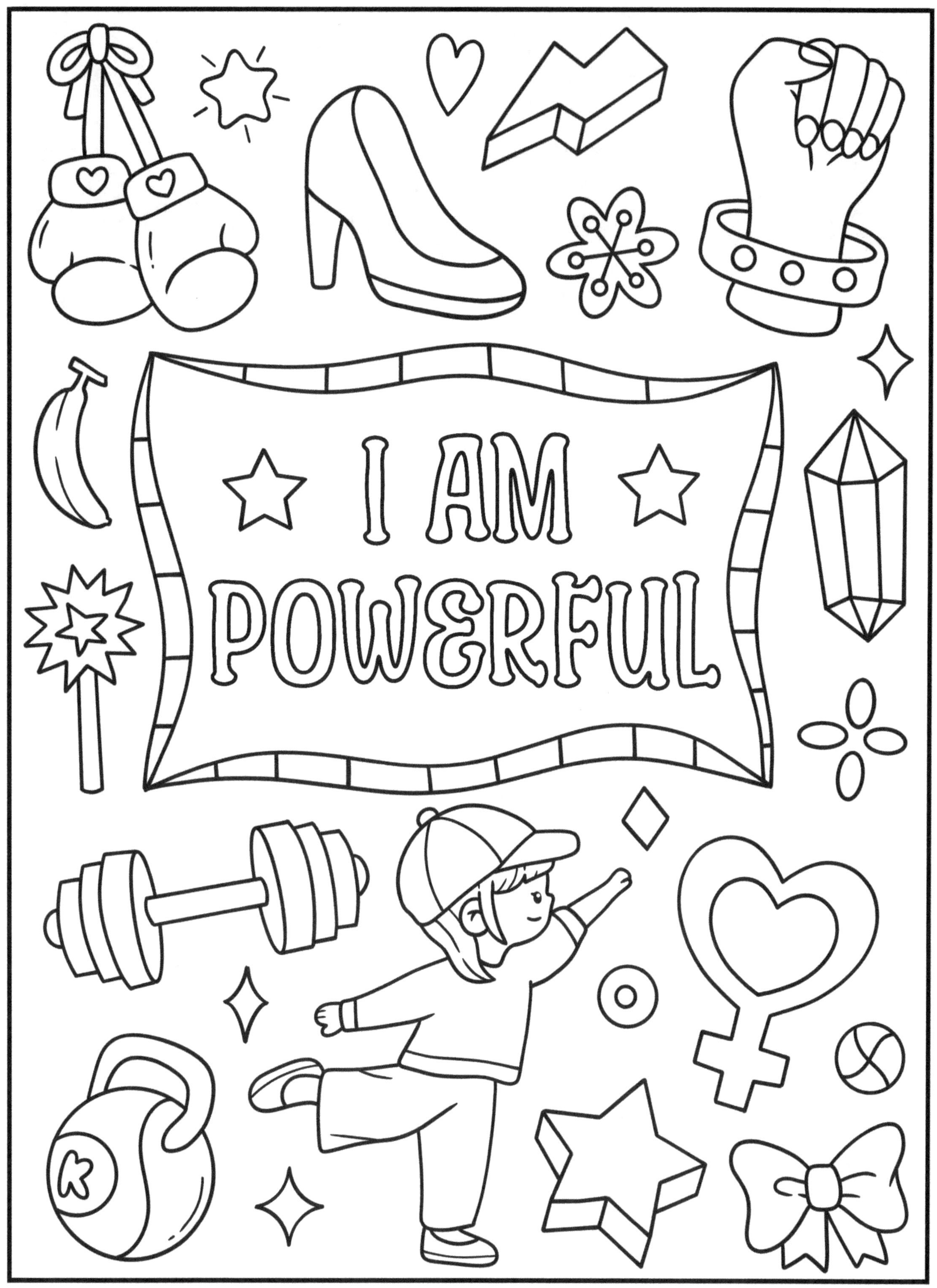
I AM
POWERFUL

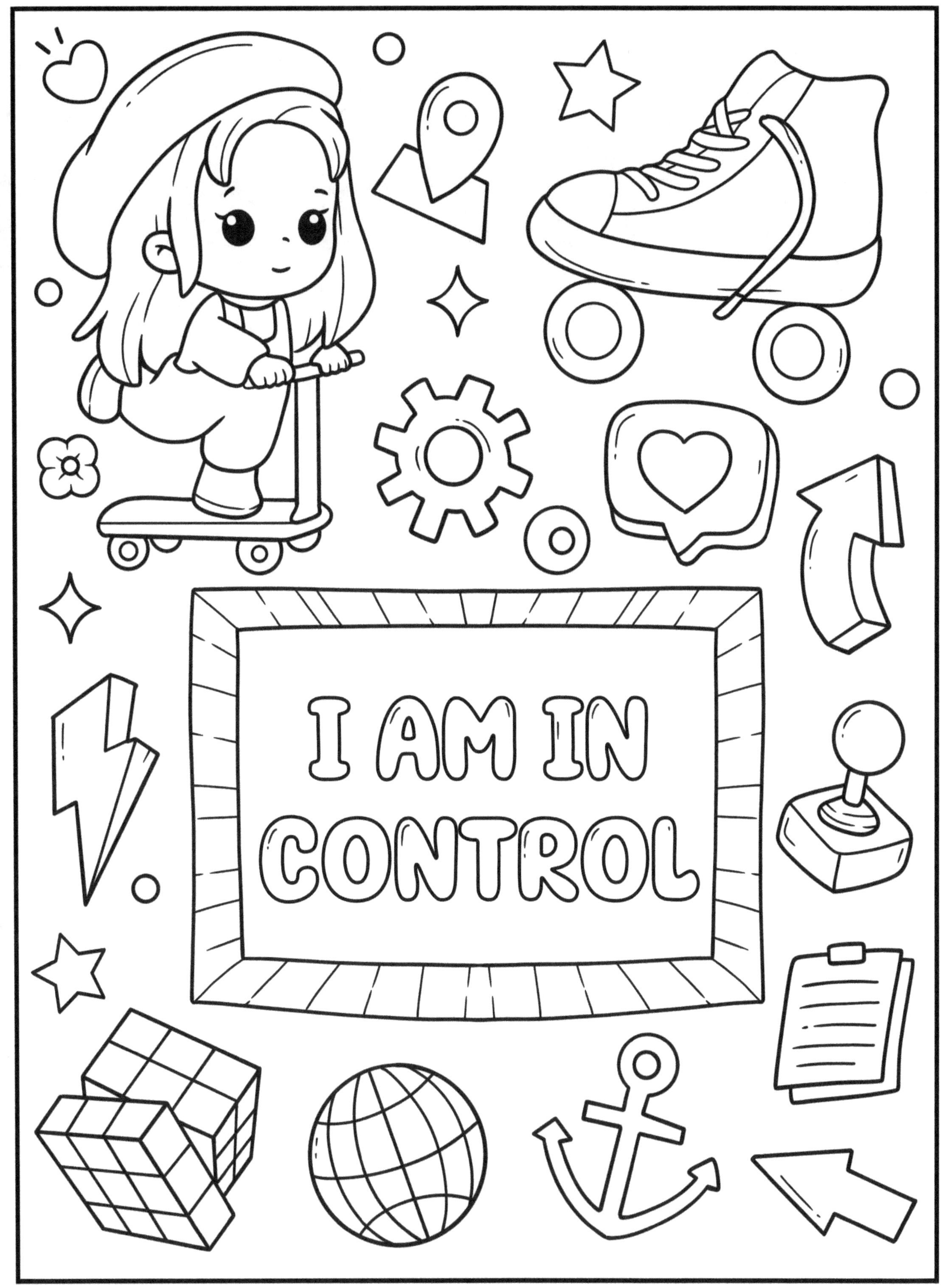
I AM IN
CONTROL

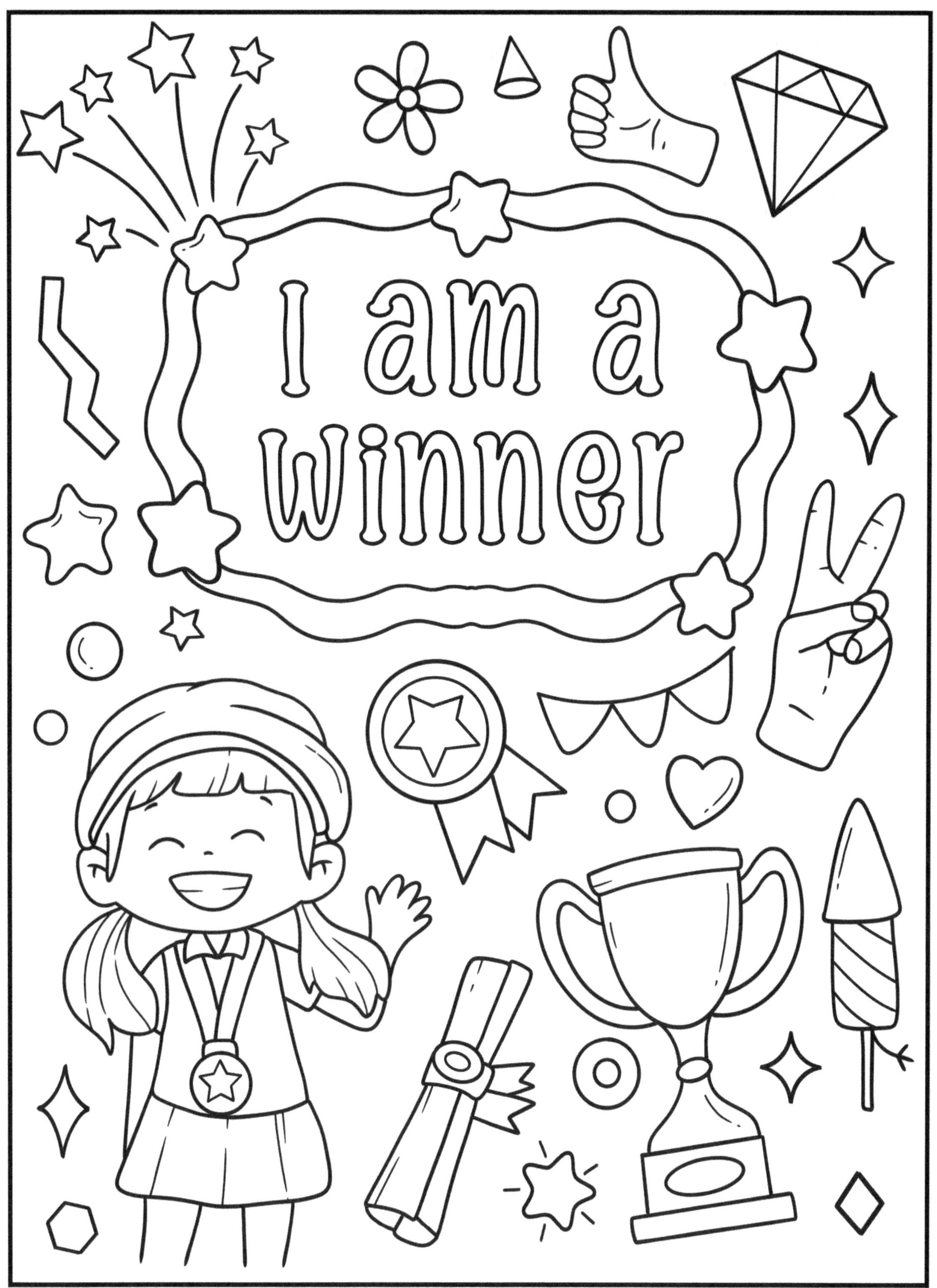
I am a
winner

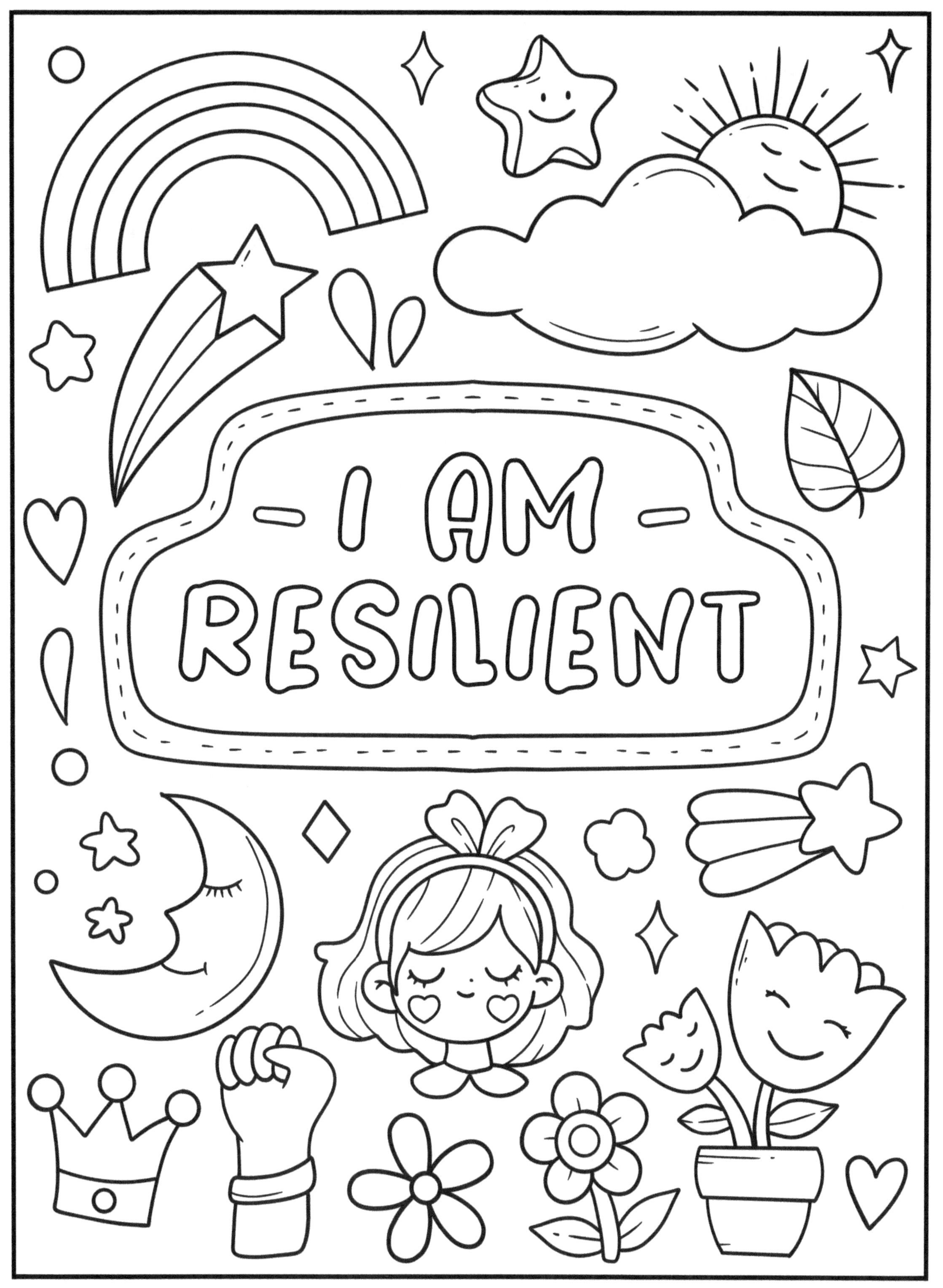
I AM
RESILIENT

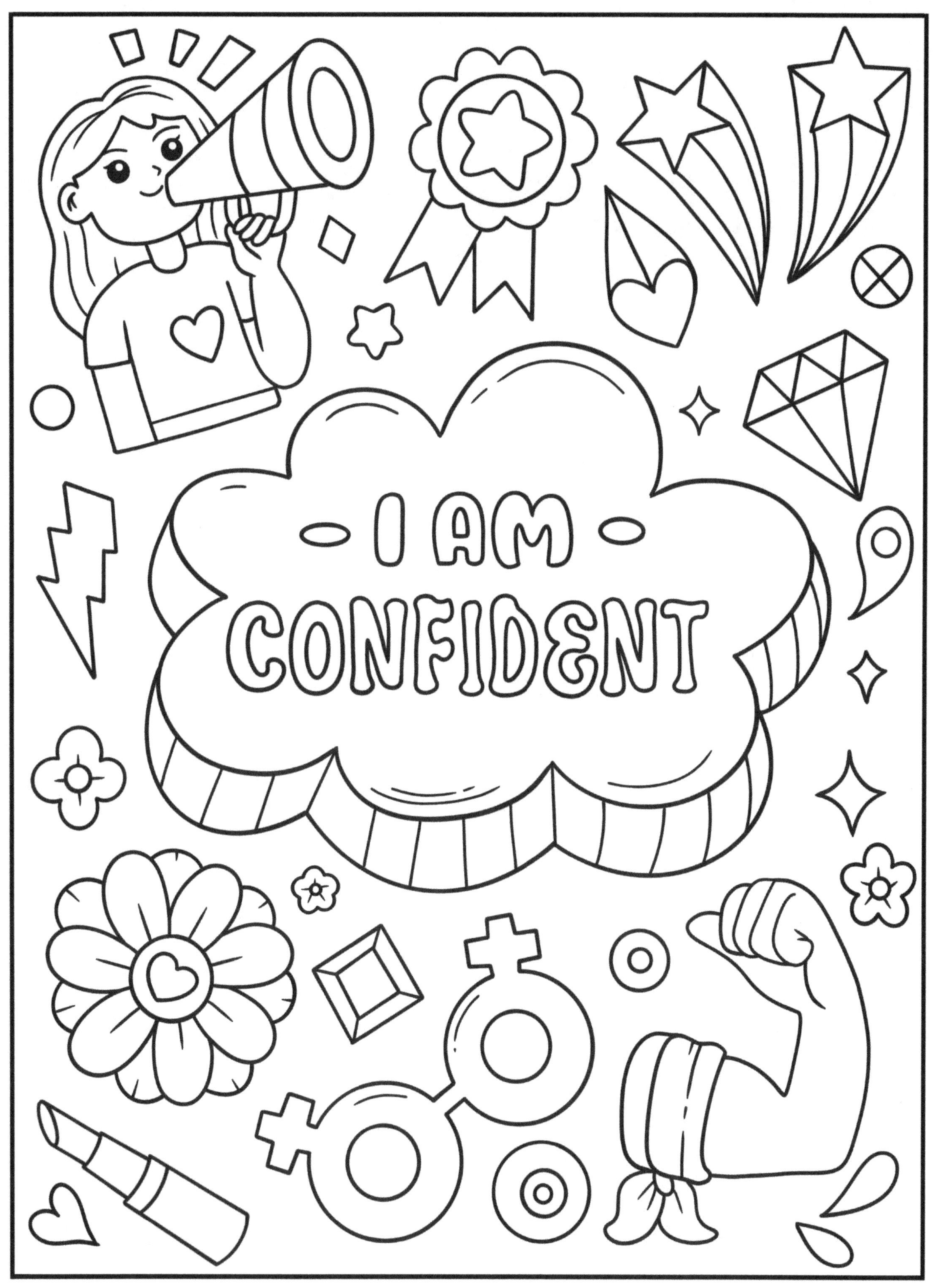
I AM
CONFIDENT

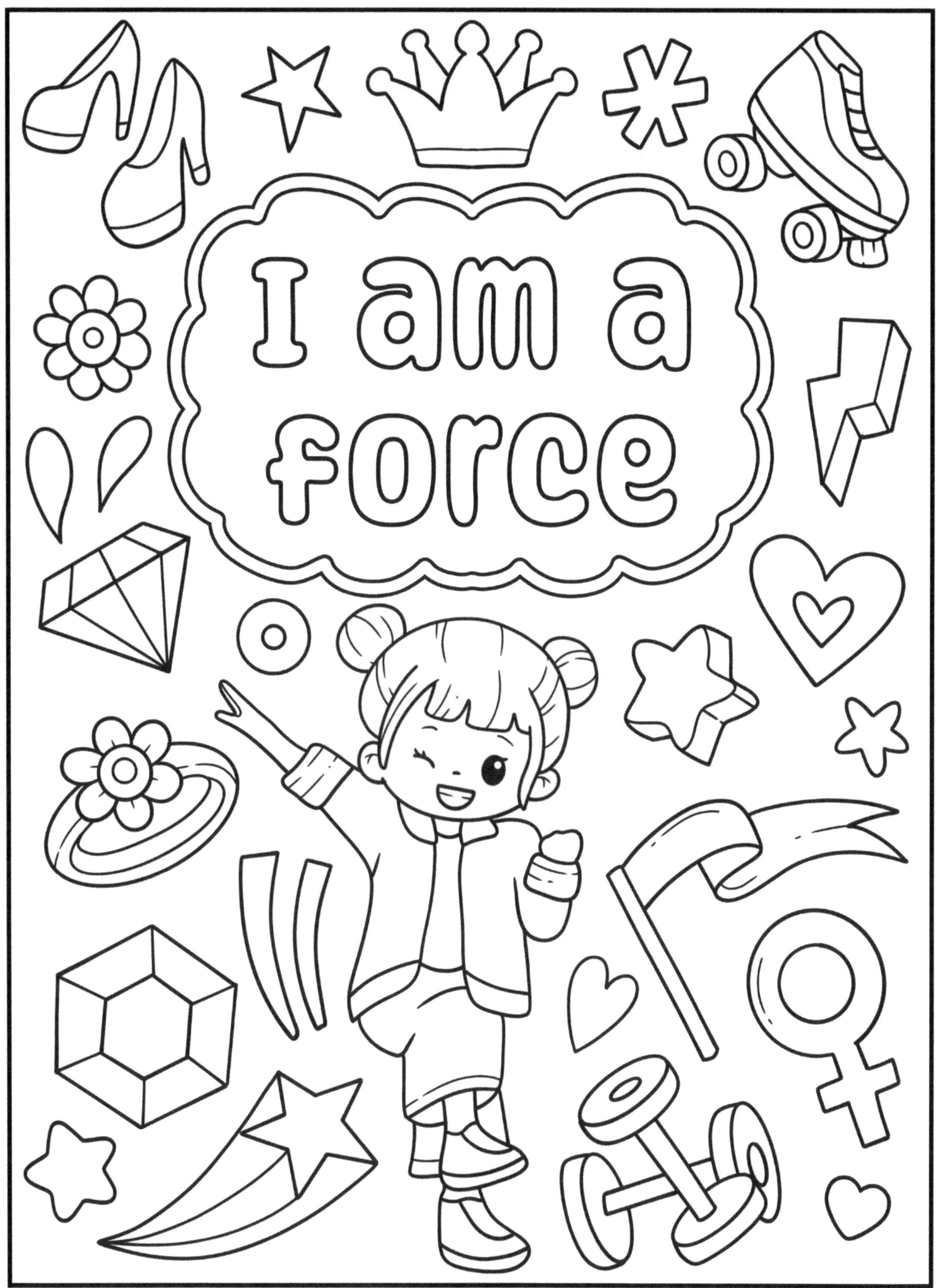
I am a force

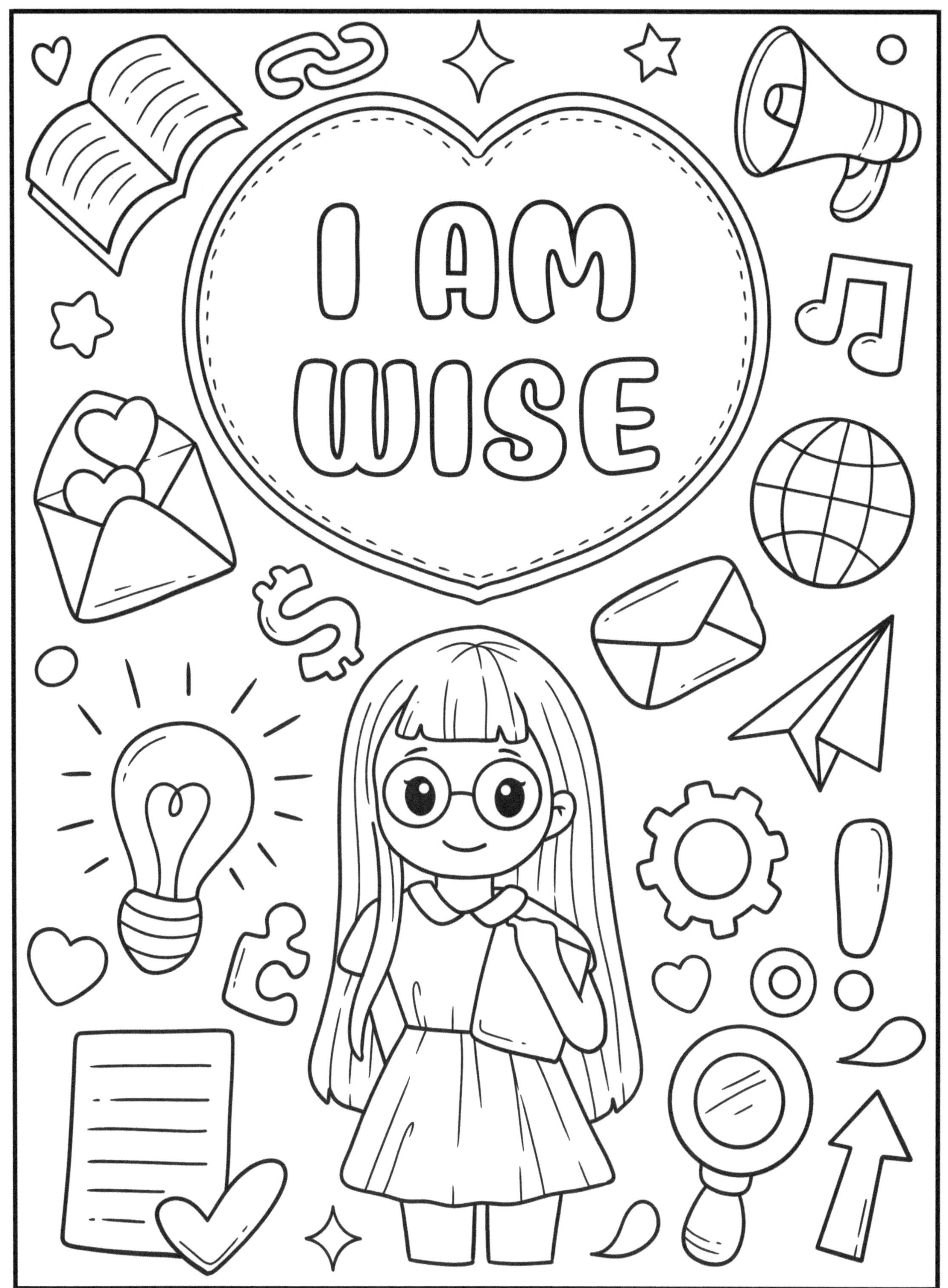
I AM
WISE

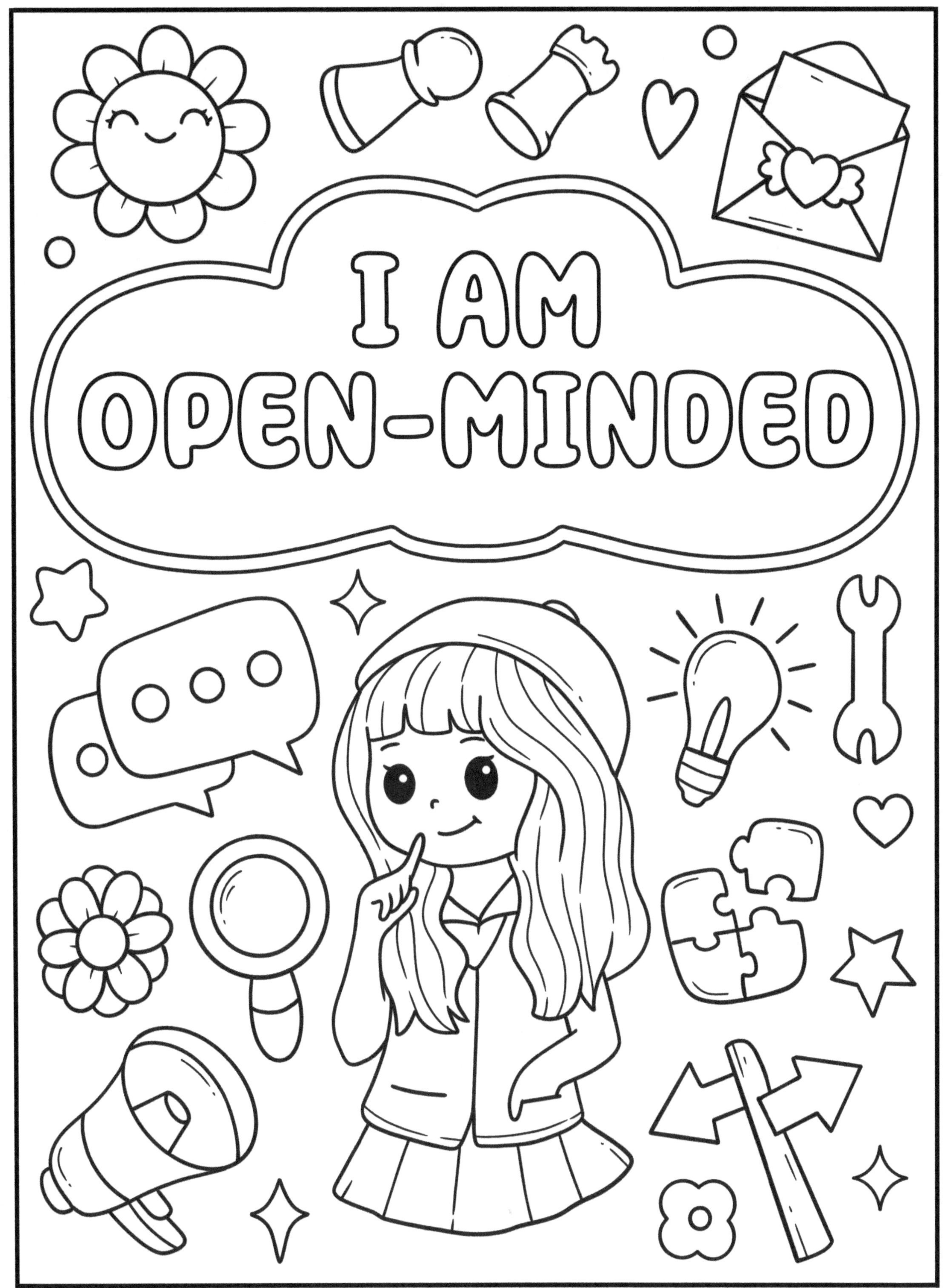
I AM
OPEN-MINDED

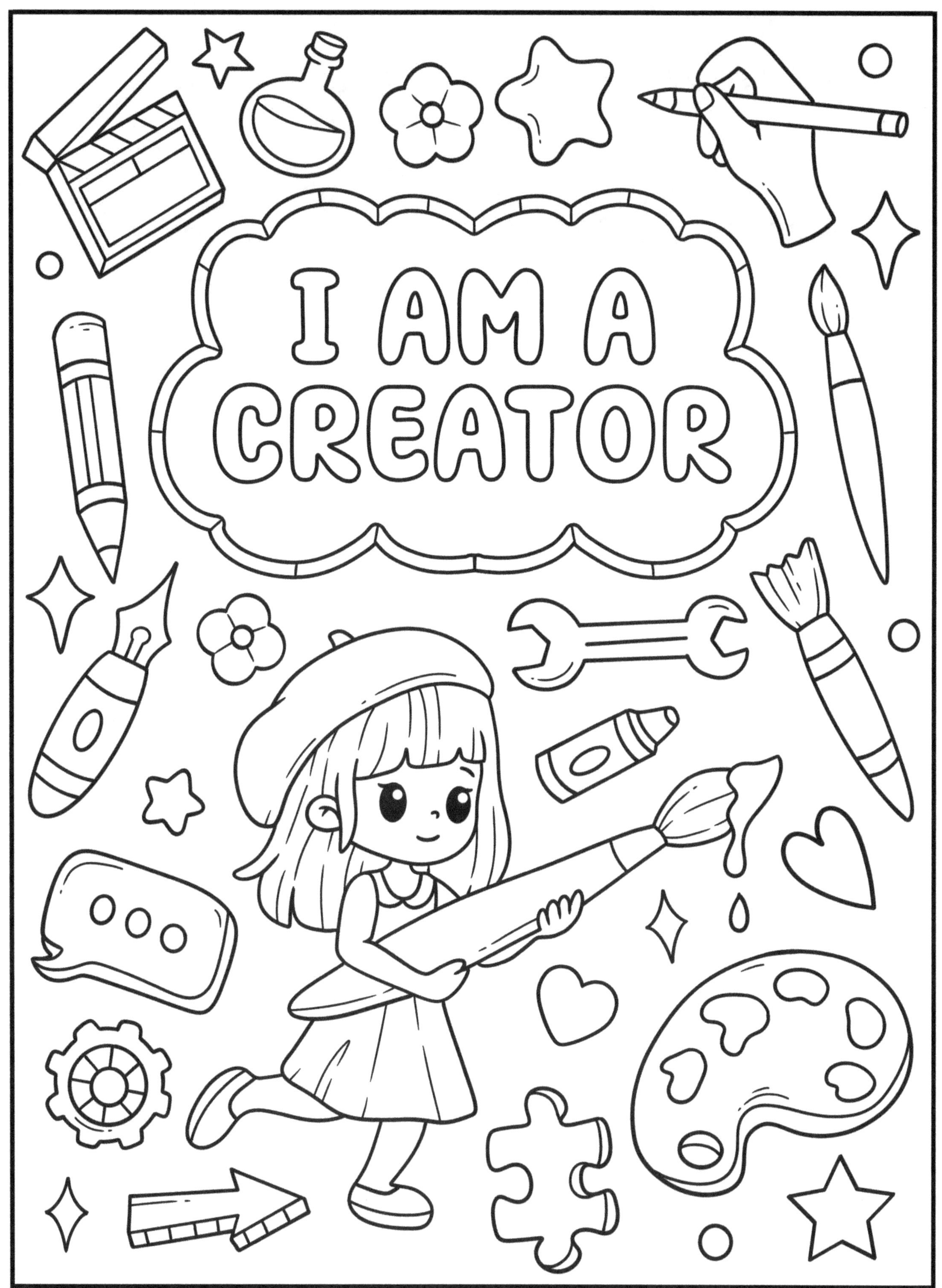
I AM A CREATOR

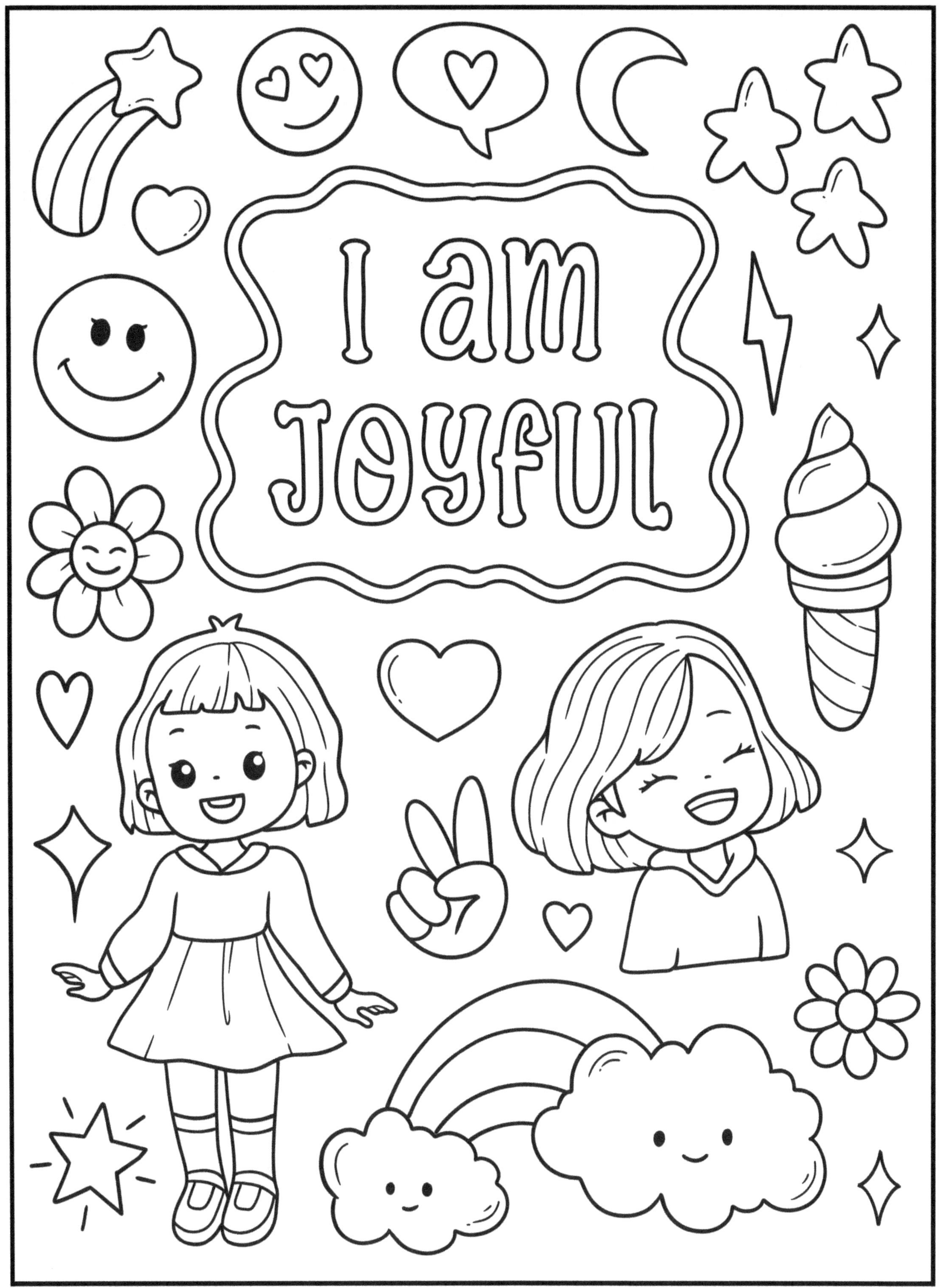
I am
JOYFUL

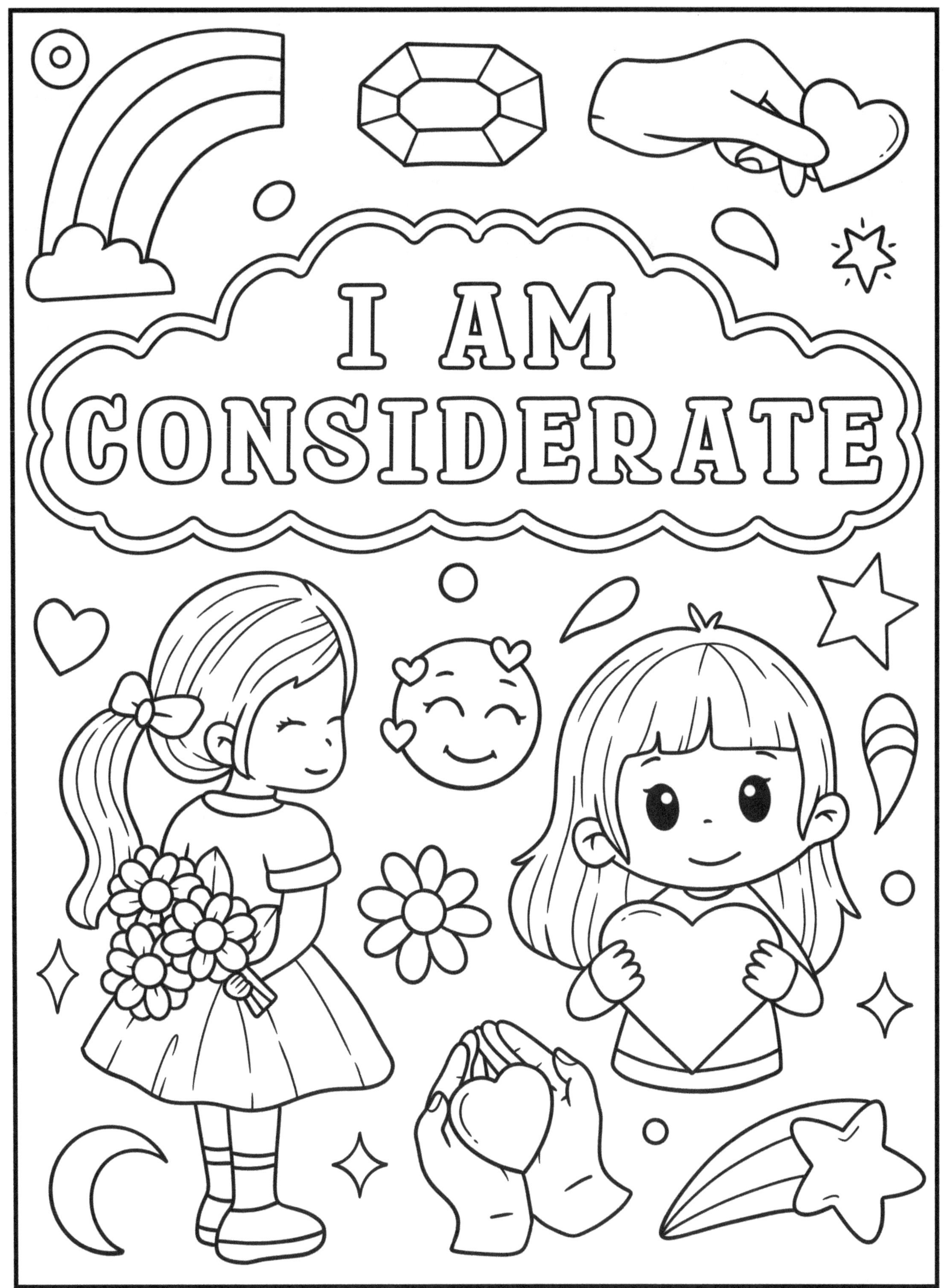
I AM
CONSIDERATE

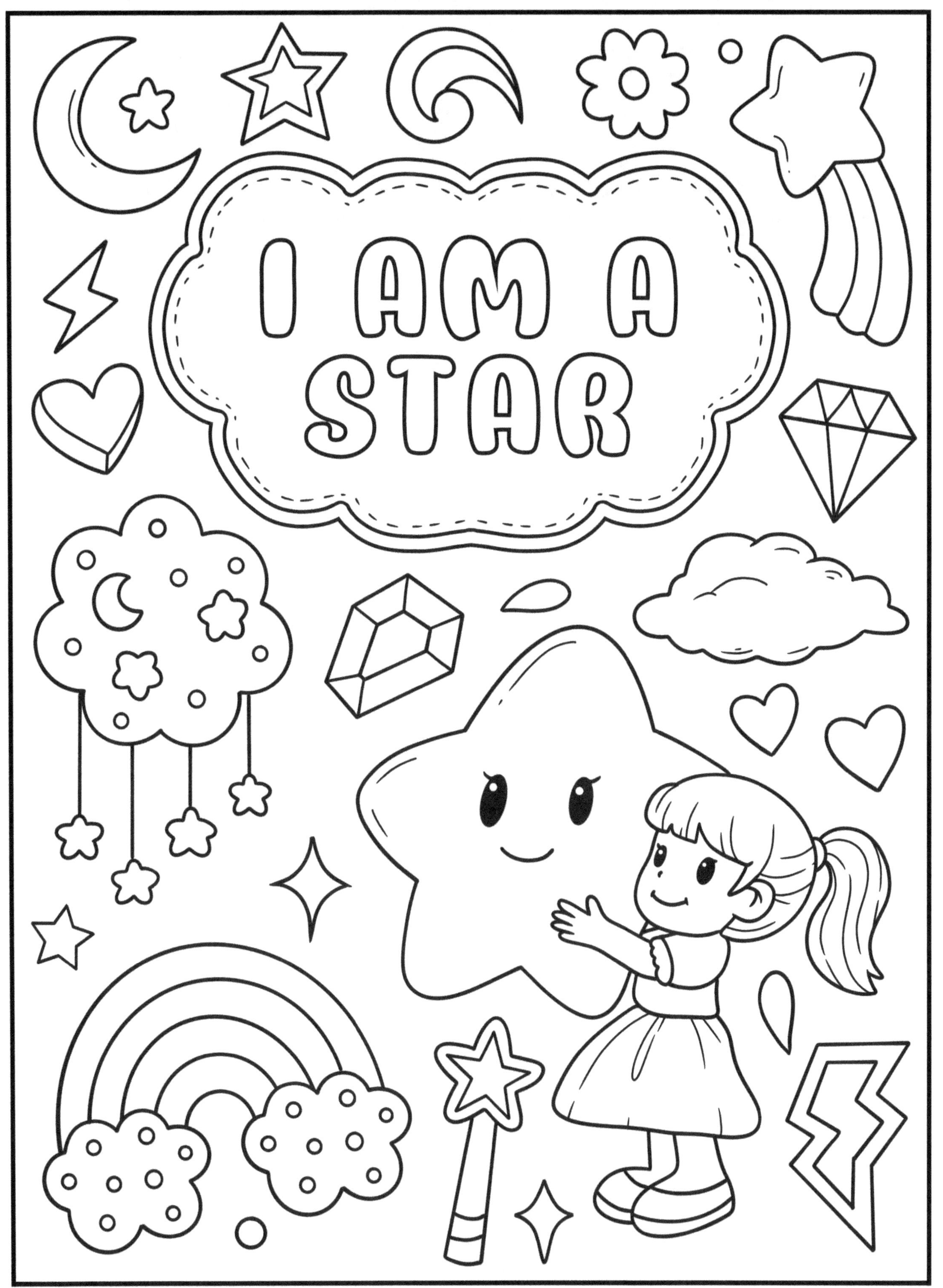
I AM A
STAR

www.ingramcontent.com/pod-product-compliance
Lightning Source LLC
LaVergne TN
LVHW061255100826
845148LV00008B/1132
9798888990339